STOP
CLUTTER
—— FROM ——
STEALING
YOUR LIFE

Discover Why You Clutter
and How You Can Stop

MIKE NELSON

NEW PAGE BOOKS
A division of The Career Press, Inc.
Franklin Lakes, NJ

STOP CLUTTER FROM STEALING YOUR LIFE
ISBN: 1-56414-502-6
Cover design by Cheryl Finbow
Printed in the U.S.A. by Book-mart Press

To order this title, please call toll-free 1-800-CAREER-1 (NJ and Canada: 201-848-0310) to order using VISA or MasterCard, or for further information on books from Career Press.

The Career Press, Inc., 3 Tice Road, PO Box 687,
Franklin Lakes, NJ 07417
www.newpagebooks.com
www.careerpress.com

Library of Congress Cataloging-in-Publication Data available upon request.

This book is dedicated to Samantha, who started me on the road to recovery, and Dana, who kept my feet on the road to happy destiny.

Contents

Introduction

I hope this book will help you free yourself from the bondage of cluttering and find your true self.

If your cluttering is causing you some difficulty, but you don't feel it is a serious issue, just use the parts of the book that relate to you and read the rest only if you like. Please don't feel that you have to be a serious hoarder to get any value out of this book. Take what you need and leave the rest.

Nearly everyone who heard I was writing a book on cluttering said, "I need that book." Most people think of themselves as clutterers in some form or another. People who are actually very neat often have closets and storage spaces filled to the brim with stuff they never use. Though it is neatly packaged, it is still clutter.

This book is for those for whom "organizing" books are not enough. It addresses cluttering as a serious challenge to living up to our full potential. The medical/psychological term for severe cases is "hoarding." This condition is considered an obsessive-compulsive disorder (OCD).

In this book, I hope to touch you with humor, love, and compassion. I am not a professional organizer, psychologist, or psychiatrist. I am just a guy who has realized that clutter has limited his life and wants to help others find the freedom he has. By interviewing professionals, self-diagnosed clutterers, and medically diagnosed hoarders, I wish to give you understanding that goes far beyond my personal experiences. I was guided to write this by my own pain and the earnest desire to help others like me get to the other side—the joy of recovery.

In this book, you will find ways to handle the feelings that cluttering produces. The book incorporates anecdotal stories about the effect of cluttering on the families of clutterers, as well as professional opinions from psychiatrists and psychologists who deal with cluttering and hoarding.

The practical, spiritual, and economic aspects of cluttering (and decluttering) are all covered, so you can see how your life can be positively changed by finding a path of recovery, whether through therapy, self-help, medication, spirituality, or a combination of any of the above.

Living a clutter-free life is more than cleaning up. It involves changing the way we think about possessions, love, and self-worth. It means developing a way of life that celebrates what we have and honors our inner self. Positivism, abundance thinking, and a spiritual way of life are both the results of, and the means to, living without clutter. A joyful, rich life is the payoff.

This is a book about freeing ourselves. We have been trapped in a prison of clutter created by a disorder called cluttering or hoarding. We are not bad or weak people any more than someone with diabetes is bad or weak. We probably own at least three books on organizing. Like Band-Aids, they have helped superficially and temporarily.

Cluttering or hoarding is not superficial or temporary. It is deep-seated and lifelong. It is a recognized psychological disorder. If you are a clutterer or hoarder, you need more than a way to organize your clutter. You want a life plan that will lead you into the sunlight of the spirit, where you can live a life without shame, self-doubt, and fear. It is my most sincere hope and belief that *Stop Clutter From Stealing Your Life* can offer these things to you.

Join me on this path to self-understanding. May we meet on the road to joy and peace.

1 | Are You A Clutterer?

"One's own self or material goods, which has more worth? Loss (of self) or possession (of goods), which is the greater evil? He who loves most, spends most, He who hoards much loses much."
—Laotse

"Get out and take your clutter with you. Maybe you can come back when you get your life under control."

With those sobering words, my former fiancée forced me to realize that cluttering is more than an annoying personality quirk. For some of us, it is a serious problem. But, as I was to discover, there is hope. Cluttering can be controlled. No matter how many books on organizing I bought, no matter how many systems I seriously applied, no matter how many professional organizers I brought into my life, the clutter controlled me, until I found the way out.

Remember the George Carlin skit about "stuff?" We need our stuff. Heck, George could have been writing the clutterer's pledge. It was funny when he did it. Everyone identifies with it. But normal people didn't leave the nightclub after Carlin's routine and have to dodge Big

Mac boxes, unfolded maps, overcoats, old clothes, magazines, and newspapers in order to get into their cars. They didn't go home to places that were so full of stuff that there was only a path through their living rooms. Clutterers live that skit every day, and the humor wanes.

I had to admit that I was different from other people, that I was powerless over my compulsion, before I could seek help and begin to recover. My life today is hundreds of times better than it was before I faced my cluttering. Cluttering is a personality dysfunction. It has nothing to do with lack of self-control or being a bad person.

Degrees of Cluttering

For most people, a desk littered with papers or a closet or garage stuffed with forgotten items is a mild annoyance. For clutterers, it is an outward manifestation of our inner lives. Inside, we are afraid of losing love, so we hang onto every object that comes into our lives. We feel that if we accumulate enough things love will magically appear. The stuff in our lives isn't the problem—the stuff in our heads is.

Don't panic. Advanced clutterers or hoarders (the medical term for a serious manifestation of out-of-control cluttering that has become an Obsessive-Compulsive Disorder) don't get cirrhosis of the liver, age prematurely, or end up in seedy thrift stores with shaking hands, begging for "just a little shot of clutter to get the day started." Or at least very few of us do. If you apply the principles set down in these pages, you'll be able to pass an entire street full of thrift shops and not even be tempted to run in for "just a peek."

Cluttering or hoarding affects a majority of the population in one way or another. There are degrees to cluttering. You don't have to have go to the extremes of some of the people you will meet in later chapters to get a lot out of this book. Even if you are just a disorganized person, you will find great insight and help overcome your slight problem before it becomes a major disability. Almost everyone I talked to when writing this book said, "Oh, I have a problem with that!" So read on before you make any judgements about how serious your cluttering is. You will be able to benefit from the experience, strength, and hope of those who went too far. Maybe you will be able to arrest what is at this point a mere annoyance with the information found here. I sincerely hope so.

Dr. Gail Steketee, the nation's leading expert on hoarding, put it into perspective for me. "For those of us who aren't suffering from psychiatric conditions, we are all suffering from flaws. We will always struggle with those things [such as weight]. We will always have to watch what we eat. We still have to be alert."

Terms

I use the term "clutterer" for the most part. "Hoarder" is a medically recognized term and applies to a condition that is serious enough to demand professional therapy and/or drug therapy. Whether you call yourself a hoarder or clutterer or packrat doesn't matter. It may be more comfortable for you to say you are a packrat. Maybe you don't have a serious problem and don't want to be identified with those who do. Only you know the truth and only you can label yourself. Whatever the case, if you follow the steps in this book, you can free yourself from cluttering.

For those of us with a serious cluttering or hoarding problem, I believe that accepting what we are—clutterers or hoarders—is more liberating than using gentler terms like "packrats" or "collectors." However, we all have to make decisions that we can live with. What is important is that we admit that we have a problem and are willing to take the steps necessary to do something about it.

Different Methods of Approach

Many different approaches are suggested in this book. I believe that there is no one solution; the treatment depends on the severity of the condition. For many, a self-help group like Clutterless or a 12-step group like Clutterers Anonymous may be enough to start and stay on the road to recovery. Others may benefit greatly from a spiritual approach. Others will require therapy. Some will benefit from medication. A cocktail of all or some of the above may work best for others. Take a look at each path, then start down the road that your heart chooses. If one approach doesn't seem to work for you, try another. Whatever you do, don't give up.

Recognizing the Problem

Some of us have turned our clutter into security blankets. We sleep on beds littered with books, clothes, papers and boxes so we don't feel so alone when we go to sleep at night. It starts with one book that we read before retiring. Then it is joined by another. It invites its friends. Before long, the books from the library are having a party on our bed, and we are just in the way.

We pile papers and books on our dining room tables until we and our families (if we still have them) have to eat from TV trays. We don't invite anyone to our houses out of shame. No one ever rides in our cars because there is only room for the driver.

In extreme cases, some of us have sold cars rather than deal with the clutter in them. We have moved rather than deal with our houses. We rent storage sheds, in ever-increasing sizes, to relieve the pressure. If enough people take the advice in this book, the storage shed industry will go on the skids—so sell your stock now.

Most of us are neat in appearance and appear normal to the outside world. Oh, maybe our desks are a little messy, but everyone laughs that off. Unlike alcoholics or drug addicts, our clutter seldom gets us fired for not showing up for work. But many of us have been fired for losing important documents, missing deadlines, missing important appointments, or screwing up our boss's travel reservations, sending her to Cancun instead of Chicago.

Stopping the Merry-Go-Round

Can we stop this black tornado of paper and useless items that swirls around us, blocking us from the sunlight of the spirit? Absolutely! It will not be easy, because no one wants to admit that he or she is not in control of every aspect of his or her life. (I will use male pronouns throughout the rest of the book simply for ease of reading, but clutterers are represented equally in both sexes).

A sober alcoholic or drug addict doesn't take alcohol or drugs into his body or house. A recovering overeater doesn't ingest more food than he needs. A recovering clutterer doesn't let clutter take back his life once he has won a few battles with it. It is a war. Clutter comes into our lives every day. We get mail that we don't need. We get bills that have to live somewhere until they are paid. Things wear out and break and get replaced by new ones. Clothes shrink (well, maybe we grow), lose buttons, fade, or go out of style. The newspaper comes every day. Eventually we learn to view these events as calls to arms. The world throws clutter at us. We learn to throw it back. Before long, you will be hitting clutter out of your life like Sammy Sosa swatting homeruns.

I've Been Where You Are

How useful is that two-legged stool in the corner of the living room? What about those old clothes choking our closets and wrinkling our good ones? Do we really need those prescriptions that expired when Reagan was president? How many of us have junk cars in our yards that we are going to restore or that might come in handy for parts? This will be bitter medicine for sports car aficionados, but even a 1965 Alfa-Romeo Spyder is a junk car when it hasn't run in 15 years.

I speak from experience. I owned that 1965 Alfa. It didn't run the day I bought it and it didn't run five years later when I sold it for $100. The stories in this book are from people just like me and you. I've had all the items above littering my life, stopping me from becoming the person I wanted to be. Yes, all this stuff really affects our personalities. It makes us shy, fearful, and angry, feeds our low self-esteem, and makes us feel "less than." So get rid of the clutter and take back control of your life!

This book is full of hope and humor. If we don't learn to laugh at our foibles, we cannot conquer them. So, my fellow clutterer, please read on. Identify with the stories in this volume and then apply their principles of recovery to your own life. You have nothing to lose but your isolation.

2 | My Story

First the good news. I (and many others like me) have gotten our cluttering under control. Although our battles will never make a Tom Clancy novel, they feel just as exciting to us. When I began writing this book, I had recycled more than 1075 pounds of paper (not including newspapers) and given away 230 pounds of books, 63 pounds of clothes, three old computers, and hundreds of floppy disks. I had thrown out a pottery pink flamingo with a broken leg, (and gave its mate to a CNN reporter who interviewed me for a story on cluttering), 10 cans of old paint, two tents without poles, and a partridge in a pear tree (just kidding about the bird). And all of that is just since I started keeping track. As a side benefit, I dropped 6 pounds, probably from carting all that stuff to the recycler.

Today my desk is clear, I can walk around any room of my house in the dark without fear of tripping, I can find a book when I need it, and

I haven't spent any time looking for my keys or wallet in a year. It took acceptance, determination, work, and the support of fellow clutterers to get this far. I am just a guy who has a problem and sought help. Thank God there are organizations of people in the same boat. I mention them so that you too can avail yourself of their support if you choose.

Helped by Self-Help Groups

One group is Clutterless, which is a self-help, not a 12-step, program (*www.clutter-recovery.com*). Anything shared there is kept confidential and is thus anonymous. Freedom to express oneself and to be heard without blame or shame are the cornerstones of this group. It is based on the principles of positive thinking, prosperity consciousness, meditation, and improving one's self-image. It can be of benefit to those who haven't gone over the top with their cluttering, as well as to those who are in therapy. It does not promote any one way of dealing with the clutter or hoarding in our lives. Sharing by clutterers or hoarders is the basis of it, but professionals, from psychologists and psychiatrists to professional organizers, ministers, and New Thought practitioners are welcome to come and present their insights.

A group based on the 12-step principles of Alcoholics Anonymous is Clutterers Anonymous (*www.clutterers-anonymous.org*). They are strictly and traditionally based on the 12 steps and 12 traditions of AA.

Different Approaches

I disagree with some organizing books in a number of areas. That isn't to say they are wrong. I can only speak from my heart and the words of those I interviewed. I don't believe in the statement, "If you haven't used it in a year (or three years, or some other arbitrary number), throw it out." If you are a clutterer, you probably couldn't find it for three years. No one can make that decision for you, and that is one thing that makes decluttering so hard.

One of our dilemmas is that our possessions give us feelings. That is what we have to deal with. Some stuff, like old love letters, family mementos, and pictures, have value. What I had to do (and this is just what worked for me) was to evaluate each of those items. At first it was hard, so I just threw them all into a box marked "memories." Later, when I had dealt with the bigger and easier stuff, I went back and sorted through the memories. In my case, about 70 percent could be discarded.

Brief Family History

I don't think I was born a clutterer, though it did run in my family. (Some research suggests there is a genetic disposition to hoarding). While decluttering my home, I had to go through many boxes of my mother's stuff. She saved a few important papers, but mostly, she saved junk. I found folder after folder of contests she entered from 1956 to 1973. However, not all saving is bad, as I also found every letter I had written to her during my vagabond youth. They were instructive and gave me a feeling of continuity.

When I was a child, I was neat. I ironed my clothes, washed dishes, and made my bed. We were poor, so I didn't have a lot of stuff to clutter up my room. I grew up on a farm, which is the devil's playground for a clutterer. The shed in back was bigger than the house and I loved it. I probably thought, "When I grow up, I'm going to become a clutterer!" Old 78 records, newspapers older than I, broken farm equipment, and assorted junk filled most of it. My father believed that everything would come in handy some day, so he kept everything. My mother ragged on him from time to time, but she had her own way of cluttering.

She filed everything. When the filing cabinets were full, she transferred the bulging folders to cardboard boxes and stored them in the garage for safekeeping. The rats ate chunks out of most of them. A good rule of thumb is that when the rats are eating better than you, it's time to start decluttering.

My first cluttering came with wheels. I got a sports car (a silver Datsun Fairlady 1500). That gave me a rationalization for keeping old spark plugs, distributor caps, and tires (you never know when you will need a spare). I justified the tires because the odd sized tires were difficult to find in 1967. The Datsun eventually broke and spent more time behind a tow truck than on the road, but I couldn't part with it.

After high school, I spent two years hitchhiking around the country and now see that my cluttering was beginning to take on unreal proportions. Unlike most hitchhikers, I carried a duffel bag because it held more stuff than a backpack. I had a sleeping bag and several changes of clothes. But why did I carry a three-pound statue of a Greek goddess? Because it was given to me by a girlfriend. I couldn't have her, so I kept a thing to give me love. Funny, that statue didn't keep me warm at night.

Wives Don't Appreciate Junk Cars or Phonebook Collections. Go figure!

When my first ex-wife (I mention the ex-wives because cluttering often got in the way of my relationships) and I moved to New Orleans, we didn't have much stuff, but we towed my broken-down sports car. All our possessions fit in the one room we rented. As we became more affluent, we rented a house. Oh boy! I got a garage!

I acquired a 1965 Alfa Romeo Spyder. It was my dream car. It didn't run, but it gave me a project to restore it. I had grown up! I had a wife, a garage, and two sports cars. I had become the clutterer I had only dreamed about being as a boy. Before long the garage was home to a broken refrigerator for beer, the Alfa, and a lot of broken tools. But, it was my garage. The broken down Datsun lived in the yard.

In college, I needed lots of books for research. I wanted to be a writer, so I had five dictionaries. Elaine (name changed to protect me from a lawsuit) bought me a new IBM Selectric typewriter. I couldn't throw the old manual one away, so I kept it for a spare—in case the electricity ever went out. But really, how likely was it that I would type by candlelight? Clutterers have all sorts of illogical excuses for keeping their junk.

Notice that there were a lot of "I" statements there. "We" didn't have a sofa, or extra chairs for guests, or a dining room table. Like most clutterers, I was self-absorbed.

I loved garage sales. Every weekend I came home with some new piece of junk. Before long we had to move to a larger house. I blamed it on the furniture my wife bought. She began to complain about my junk encroaching on her space. I think it was the collection of phonebooks from every major city in the United States, Mexico, Canada, and France that finally did her in. Our arguments often ended with, "Take your junk and get out."

It was 30 years until I really heard that statement. After all, I was an artist. I was allowed to be eccentric.

Bachelorhood = More Clutter

The marriage ended, but I can't blame it all on my cluttering. My active alcoholism and irresponsibility had a lot to do with it. Very few wives would have understood why I wanted to quit college and become a jungle explorer (which I did eventually become). I moved into a small furnished apartment. It was crammed wall to ceiling with books and junk. I was happy. My possessions gave me a feeling of security and love. My bed was a minefield. There was barely enough room for me. Several girlfriends came over and tried to help me "get organized." Fortunately for them, there was no way for two people to get into the bed at the same time. They usually gave up on the project and me after a couple of weeks. For solace, I went to more garage sales and carted home more junk.

A Billboard?

The most bizarre thing I accumulated was a billboard. In a bourbon-induced haze, three friends and I stole it in some small Louisiana town. I took it with me to Memphis and back to New Orleans a year later. You should have seen the looks on the mover's faces.

It was a look that I saw more and more frequently as I grew older. Without saying a word, people conveyed amazement and disgust at the way I lived. I had no shame and invited people to my house.

Once, my apartment was burglarized. When the cops saw my living room, they said, "Man, they really did a number on this place." In fact, the burglars hadn't touched a thing in my living room. That was the way it normally looked.

I had always had a golden touch and was able to make a lot of money at executive positions. At work, I was a neat freak. My desk was always cleared when I went home. I made to-do lists. I was the model of efficiency.

My cluttering downfall came when I went into business for myself as a stock trader in the 1980s. The Internet was in its infancy, so I had a ticker tape, which consumed rolls of yellow paper, best suited for throwing out the window during parades. New Orleans had a lot of parades, but I kept that ticker tape. My closet began to fill. I had to save *The Wall Street Journal, Barron's,* and *The New York Times* for "research."

When I went bust and moved, I left behind an entire room full of old papers and ticker tapes. I was sure that someone else would appreciate the valuable library. All I took with me fit into the back of a pickup truck. I hope my irate ex-landlord doesn't read this. Actually, I have to make amends to him, something that comes with recovery.

I then lived clutter-free in a one room house in Mexico. I owned nothing but a duffel bag and a few books. When I left a year later, I left behind a clutter mess. Poor people in Mexico hang on to everything that crosses their path. There was a difference, though—they used those things. I just collected them.

I returned to the U.S. with only a half-full duffel bag and lived in a furnished room in Seattle. My fortunes increased again, and so did my stuff. I moved to sunny Southern California. By the time I left San Diego, I had to rent a storage space for my stuff.

One clue that I was out of control again should have been when I had to hire a moving company to transport my junk from California to my mother's home in Texas. She, the ultimate clutterer, said, "How did you ever collect so much junk?"

Married to a Neat Freak

Then I married a compulsive neat freak. That is common with clutterers. We often marry people for whom our clutter will cause conflicts. We do so in the hopes that their neatness, which we equate with goodness, will rub off on us. It doesn't. They just get frustrated and angry. Many clutterers have unhappy spouses and think the problem with their lives is their spouse. "If only he or she would stop nagging, life would be perfect."

Lost Job Due to Cluttering

I garnered a dream job writing guidebooks to Mexico, which I then lost, to a large degree, because of my cluttering. Because I was a recognized eccentric and artist, I cluttered my office with papers and books and statuary. The six-foot wooden doorjambs from Michoacán, Mexico, were probably the most bizarre. How I got away with it, heaven only knows. A reporter for a news magazine interviewed me and couldn't take a picture of me behind my desk because everything was piled too high. He took the shot outside. When new management came in, they started their decluttering with me.

Moving Didn't Help

Thinking a change of address would help, I tried to sell my house to move back to Los Angeles. It took six months to sell. People came in, and although I had done what I thought was an exemplary job of stuffing things into my garage, they were appalled. Books (a common clutter problem—we just can't part with the written word), overflowed the shelves, papers were jammed everywhere, and it was always an adventure when prospective buyers opened a closet door. One lady was actually covered in an avalanche of papers and audio tapes that fell on her head when a sagging shelf collapsed.

To move, I rented a small U-Haul trailer. Clutterers often have a poor sense of space utilization. After three more trips to U-Haul, each time getting a bigger trailer, I had to get a Ryder truck. I got the biggest truck available. It wasn't big enough. When the guys started loading it, they gave me that now very familiar look. I left half a garage and a pickup truck behind, as I had two cars again. This time my Alfa ran, though.

The move cost me $2,000. Had I decluttered before I left, it would have cost me about $400. My clutter was now causing me financial losses.

The end was near. I rented a two-bedroom apartment and had to pay $300 a month extra for the second bedroom just to store all my things. I stopped inviting people to my home. My truck was just as bad.

The Dawning of Recovery

When I met my last fiancée, I was able to keep her away from my apartment for three months. I'm surprised she didn't think I was married. Whenever we went anywhere, we went in her car, as my truck was too cluttered. I moved to her place. When she finally saw my apartment, she, too, gave me "The Look." But she was a kind person and thought she could help me. She tried to do it herself. When it was obvious that either the relationship or my clutter had to go, she hired a professional organizer. The organizer estimated that it would cost at least $1,000 just to get a good start at cleaning up the wreckage of my present.

Gradually, my stuff overflowed into my beloved's neat house. At first I had space in her closet. Then I got my own closet. Then we bought a portable closet for the garage. By the end, I had taken over her extra bedroom. Finally, she too gave up on me.

Hitting Bottom

What sane man would choose stacks of useless items over a beautiful woman who loved him?

My business suffered. I missed deadlines because I couldn't find papers. It took too much research to find my research notes. Even with the Internet, I couldn't find files I needed because of the clutter in my computer. My income spiraled downward. I was alone and broke. It all seemed hopeless.

That's when I found a self-help group. When I first heard of it, I refused to go. I thought it was a silly California over-the-top self-help group for the terminally needy.

After a few more weeks of despair, I went. That's when I found out that I was not the only person with this problem. Others had stories that made mine seem insignificant. Some just had minor disorganization difficulties. Most were somewhere in between. Most importantly, some had actually made progress in their battle with cluttering. They had been to the same abyss as I and had come back to live lives that were clutter free. One of their tenets is that we clear ourselves of negative thinking when we clear ourselves of clutter.

Once I accepted that I was powerless over my cluttering behavior and that with the help of a Higher Power I could clean up my life, things got better. As I decluttered, my mind began to work better. The depression lifted. I felt more productive.

Suze Orman, the financial guru who has helped millions attain financial independence, addresses clutter in her books, *The Courage To Be Rich* and *Nine Steps to Financial Freedom*. She says that having too much stuff keeps wealth from flowing into your life. According to Science of Mind (a religion—not to be confused with Christian Science or Scientology—based on the philosophy that people are inherently good and are expressions of God), you have to make room in your life for the good to flow in. You must get rid of negative thoughts and things and replace them with positive ones. You cannot hold on to your mistakes.

Katherine Ponder, a spiritual prosperity writer, says clutter holds us back from our ultimate good. Our outside is a reflection of our state of mind.

All of these wonderful writers delivered the same message. I finally got it.

Thus began my recovery. It is a never-ending journey that has hills and valleys and curves. There are times when clutter creeps back into my life. When it does, so does depression, negative thinking, and confusion. Fortunately, I now have the tools to fight back and each bout of recidivism lasts a shorter time. The ideas in this book are universal. Many of them are practical common sense. Others address the inner states of mind that our clutter causes. Join me in this journey and you will find that your life will become richer and more fulfilling. And you do it one piece of useless junk at a time.

3 | Common Clutterer Traits

"There is no single cause. It would be easier to treat if there were one cause. You have addictive savers, similar to people who are addicted to alcohol or overeating. They do it to numb out bad feelings....Another type of clutterer is frugal. They have a strong rationale for everything they save....[The third type] are people who have an enormous problem making decisions and they can't stay focused....The fourth type suffers from Obsessive-Compulsive Disorder."

—Lynda Warren, San Bernadino psychologist,
in a 1994 *Long Beach Press-Telegram* interview

W hy do we clutter or hoard? Most of us have a combination of personality traits that contribute to our cluttering. However, no matter what reasons there are for your personal cluttering, eliminate the following excuses. "I am an artist. Artists are messy." "I am a genius (Einstein was a clutterer). We are allowed." "I am a Latvian (or any nationality). It is part of my culture."

Just to review, there is no difference between someone who calls himself a clutterer or a packrat. Both are self-diagnosed terms. A hoarder is someone who has a medically recognized personality disorder (see Chapter 6 for a discussion of this). A collector is someone who keeps memorabilia or sets of items that are related to each other. Collectors can be hoarders or clutterers, but not all hoarders or clutterers are collectors, though they may rationalize their disorder by calling it a collection. When I collected phonebooks and bottle caps, I was cluttering. When I collected stamps and coins, I was collecting.

The question each of us must answer is whether we need therapy or whether a self-help group or 12-step program is enough. Some of us can develop the self-awareness necessary to overcome this challenge without therapy; others cannot. For some, a combination of a self-help group and therapy works well (see Chapter 6). Willingness to change is necessary in either case. It has been stated several times in the medical literature that a person who doesn't want to change will have limited results from therapy. Ya gotta wanna.

1. Insecurity

This is probably the root cause. We keep useless stuff because we are afraid that there won't be any more for us. We cling to the things we have (including relationships), even if they are broken, because we don't feel we deserve any better. Our rationalizations include: "Saving for a rainy day;" "Waste not, want not;" "A penny saved is a penny earned;" or some other platitude from *Poor Richard's Almanac*. "Poor" Richard was rich Ben Franklin, and those sayings were a product of the Puritan beliefs of the time. Back then, goods were in short supply and people really did "fix it up, use it up, or wear it out." Today we don't have to.

Be honest. Are you really going to fix that broken vase? Do you even know where the glue is? If you could find it, could you get the cap off? It's not the vase. It's the fear that we'll never get another one, or that we don't deserve anything better. There are never enough things to fill that hole in our guts.

2. Feeling Unloved

We fill our lives with things to replace the love we don't feel we are getting or didn't get a long time ago. Even if we have loving spouses (and it takes a lot of love to live with a clutterer), we are afraid we will lose them or are not worthy of them, so we get more things. But things don't love you; only people love you. That teddy bear with the missing eye and stuffing falling out (I got rid of mine last year) doesn't love you. It was an expression of love from the person who gave it to you. But you can carry that love in your heart. Bury the bear. Nobody wants a ratty old bear.

3. Feeling Less Than

We feel like we are not as good, smart, pretty, and so on as other people. So we fill our lives with stuff to make us feel better. Our junk doesn't make us any "more than." If we took an inventory (ugh!) of all our stuff and carried it with us, do you think it would make anyone think any more of us? Imagine going to a party and holding out the list of your junk, saying, "Hi, my name is Sally and this is who I am." We are not our stuff.

Instead of an inventory of your possessions, why not make an inventory of your inner stuff? What are your best qualities? Your greatest assets may not be things you have done, but the person you are. To start with, you are the only living being qualified to be you. If you are kind and loving, you should celebrate that. If you have done others good turns in life, that makes you a contributor to the betterment of mankind. We can't all be Mother Teresa, but we can all make a difference in at least one person's life. We all have, if we think about it. If nothing springs to mind immediately, you can say, "When I am really happy, I like to _____." You may like to go to museums, and that makes you good at appreciating art. You may like to fish, and that brings to mind your successes in fishing. You may get pleasure from gardening. That could be one of your best qualities. The list goes on and on, and so do your good qualities.

We weren't always this way. We may be so down on ourselves that we have to go back to childhood to find a time we excelled at something. Maybe we played the saxophone well as a kid. It doesn't matter if we were first chair or seventh chair, we played it better than those who never tried. When I did this exercise, I started playing the sax again.

4. Listening to Old Tapes

Many of us were told we were no good, would never amount to anything, or as a Woody Guthrie song says, "too old, too fat, too thin, too this or too that." Chances are, we were told this when we were children. We aren't children anymore. Let's let those people go and stop giving them power over us.

Often there are people in our lives today who give us the same negative talk. They may not realize the power their words have on us. Until we get the courage to ask them to stop, we can learn to discount their negative statements. We are not alone. Ann Landers and Dear Abby columns are filled with people with this same problem. If this comes from a spouse, maybe our cluttering is contributing to the negativity. Quite possibly, we are giving ourselves this same negative talk.

Most of us have the habit of beating ourselves up. But we can begin to change that right now. When we catch ourselves putting ourselves down, we can learn to say, "Wait, that's not true. I am really good at _____." We may not believe it at first, but if we say it often enough, we will. As time goes on, we will remember more and more things we are good at.

5. Needing to Save for a "Rainy Day"

We were taught the rainy day concept by our parents. What if there is a shortage, or another depression? What if we lose our jobs? What if the sky falls? Those "what ifs" are keeping us from enjoying a full life right now.

Sometimes, the "what ifs" happen. But instead of ruining our lives, they can enhance them. I live in Galveston, Texas, which in September, 1900, was the second most important port in the United States. Then the most devastating hurricane in American history leveled the entire city, killing 6,000 people. The docks were out of commission for years, and nearby Houston eclipsed it as a port. Instead of asking "What if the storm hadn't hit us?" residents refocused their vision. Instead of becoming just another seaport, it became a very independent-thinking

city that led to a colorful and exciting history. If Galveston had suc-
cumbed to despair, it would have slipped into oblivion. Instead, it found
its true nature and became what it is today. The residents celebrate its
uniqueness. If an entire city can refocus, we can too.

Our parents did the best they could in raising us. They suffered
through a depression, or if you are younger, a couple of recessions. Fear
and scarcity ruled their lives. But you are not your parents. We live in a
world that is substantially different than theirs. There is great abundance in the world. More importantly, there is great abundance in you.
I believe that when you believe in lack, you experience lack. When you
believe in abundance, your life will be filled with as much love and
prosperity as you can handle. It's really your choice.

Suze Orman addresses this same issue. She is as practical as they
come, so even if you don't believe in the abundance principle, listen to
her. Suze says save, don't squirrel. Besides, squirrels save nuts. And you
aren't saving nuts, are you? (Are you?!) Suze points out practical ways to
save money and to put it to work for you. She writes that money flows,
and that if we block the flow of it, it will cease flowing to us.

My favorite practical spiritual author, Katherine Ponder, writes in
The Dynamic Laws of Prosperity, calling it the "Vacuum law of prosperity."
She says, "The vacuum law of prosperity is one of the most powerful,
though it takes bold faith to put it into operation....If you want great
good, greater prosperity in your life, start forming a vacuum to receive
it. In other words, **get rid of what you don't want to make room for
what you do want**."

This has been demonstrated over and over again in my life, sometimes in immediate ways. I found $1,100 the first time I decluttered.
The second time yielded $730. The third netted me $260. How much
more good would that cash have done me if I used it to pay off high-
interest bills? Or done something fun like going on a vacation? Recently, I took my penny jar to a coin machine to cash it in. Yes, I got a
windfall of $87.23, but I had to pay 10 percent for the privilege. Pretty
sorry money management, don't you think?

Hoarders routinely buy two, three, or a dozen of everything. Two-
for-one sales are our downfall. We turn them into four-for-two sales. As
I have decluttered, I've found enough file folders, labels, pens, staplers,
and so on to start a stationery store. Those things had value, but they
cost me more than they were worth in storage and confusion. What

good are spares if you cannot find them when you need them? I still have them, but they are neatly placed where I can find them when I need them. And I have used them.

Those of us who grew up poor have a real problem with this. We didn't have anything growing up and want to make up for it now. As children, we never had enough to throw away. Now we are adults on the outside, but still scared little kids inside. We can gently grow up and claim our adulthood.

We could be laid off tomorrow. I have been laid off several times. My 12 pairs of scissors, three old computers, seven staplers, and boxes of God knows what didn't cushion the blow. They didn't make me feel rich. When I came to believe in abundance, I realized that better jobs and situations always came along.

If you use something, then of course buy the economy size—if you have room. I have a tiny freezer and just can't. Learn to accept the reality of your circumstances. I feel like you can never have enough toilet paper, so I buy it in packages that defy the imagination. When I had a publishing business, I used Styrofoam peanuts to ship books, so I bought the biggest sack available. It was so big that I couldn't put it in my car, so I returned to the store in my truck. I've moved twice since then and still had enough peanuts to feed a circus' worth of Styrofoam elephants. In the last move, my friend who came to help me said, "I hate these things. We're getting bubble wrap." So I tossed them.

6. Feeling Overwhelmed

This is common when we try to face our cluttering. There's a good reason for it—it is overwhelming if we look at the whole mess. It didn't get this way overnight. What do we expect, that a genie will come in and make it all go away in eight hours? Think about how long it took to accumulate all that stuff. Then be thankful that it won't take as long to get rid of it, though it may seem that way.

As Teddy Roosevelt said, "Do what you can, with what you have, where you are." The important thing is that we start. Many have found it best to start with something manageable that will show the results of our efforts quickly. Sometimes, in a self-defeating frame of mind, we begin decluttering with a drawer. I know others have suggested this. All I know is that for me, attacking something that I walk around or push aside every day has more immediate impact than a drawer that I won't see once it is closed.

Our hoarding is an outward manifestation of our inward feelings. By leaving the visible clutter for later, we just keep reinforcing our feelings of powerlessness. So clear a spot of floor or a square of desk space and then stand back and admire it. Seeing wood or carpet is often a clutterer's first phrase of recovery.

7. Feeling Guilty

We're in a real bind here. We feel guilty because we have all this junk, and we feel guilty if we throw it away. If it's something that Aunt Tillie gave us, we feel we're being disloyal to her memory if we get rid of it. Never mind that the hula dancer with the clock in her belly is hideous. She brought it all the way from Honolulu. Never mind that the beer stein in the shape of Santa Claus is ugly and awkward to drink out of, Uncle George went to a lot of trouble to bring it back from Germany.

So what?

They may be dead and won't notice that you don't have it anymore.

They may have forgotten all about it.

If it means so much to them, do they have one on their mantle?

No matter how bad their taste may have been, they brought you a gift. They may have put a lot of thought into it, or they may have grabbed it at the airport before they left. Either way, you'll never know and it doesn't matter today. Mentally thank them for it and toss it, or give it to a charity. Some other poor hoarder or collector may be pining away for it. The kind thing, though, would be to smash it and then toss it. You aren't saying you love them any less.

8. Feeling Like a Failure

Before we confronted our clutter, we felt "less than." Once we start thinking about doing something about it, we may feel like failures. Don't worry. This is a sign of recovery. Feelings of failure when confronting our clutter are common. After I'd cleared my bedroom to the point that anyone would be proud to sleep there and cleaned my office until it sparkled, I still got blindsided by failure feelings. When I went into my second bedroom and saw the piles and piles of junk, I felt like I hadn't done anything at all. I went into a tailspin and the next thing I knew, my desk was cluttered and piles of clothes and books started sprouting on my bed.

We are going to have setbacks. We did not become perfect when we started to clean up our mess. If we don't have a support group like "Clutterless" *(www.clutter-recovery.com)* where we will find other clutterers who have been where we are, or a therapist, we find a friend who will listen to us non-judgmentally. The important thing is that we don't let these feelings of failure take root and grow and that we don't isolate.

9. Feeling Confused

Mental clutter is common. When we first start to face our problem, chances are we are walking around in a mental fog. Lynda Warren, a San Bernadino psychologist, describes clutterers as "people who have an enormous problem making decisions and [who] can't stay focused."

We forget things. We may be worried that Alzheimer's is sneaking up on us even though we are relatively young. But cheer up! None of my research indicated a correlation between Alzheimer's and cluttering.

When I was in the throes of my cluttering, it was difficult to keep an assistant for my home offices. The more cluttered my office, the less time they stayed. Each said he felt like he was descending into a black hole when he came to work. If they felt this way being here only a few hours a day, imagine what it did to me.

It's a chicken and egg thing. Which do you get rid of first—the cluttered mind or the cluttered life? Although the physical clutter is probably the first thing you should attack, don't forget about your mind. I've found that visualization and meditation help. I visualized a clutter-free home long before I had one. Visualize exactly what your beautiful, neat living room will look like when you are done. Then imagine the looks of surprise and pleasure on the faces of those you invite over to celebrate your success.

Remember the spiritual key: G.O.D.—Good Orderly Direction. Visualizing and meditating on peace and order will give your confusion a rest, and the direction to tackle the disorder will flow. If you are unfamiliar with visualization or meditation techniques, there are many books on the subject. You can find them at metaphysical bookstores and even many mainstream bookstores.

Of course, faith without work is dead, so don't just imagine what your home will look like. You still have to do the work, but it will become surprisingly easier after you have envisioned it.

10. Feeling There Is Not Enough Time

Ah, the time trap. If we are vague about everything else in our lives, why should time be any different? We often have a poor sense of time and miss deadlines—not because we can't do the work, but because we forgot the deadline date. We wake up one day and there is a due date for some project unforgivingly staring at us from our calendar.

We don't keep track of time and don't prioritize. We get distracted by other projects and don't allow enough time for them.

So, what to do? Well, the old standby, a to-do list, helps. For clutterers, however, it has drawbacks. We have to put deadlines on it, yet still make it flexible enough to allow for the added projects that we know we will tackle. That is part of our nature, and instead of rigorously adhering to the conventional wisdom of what works for other people, we should adapt their programs to our personalities.

A common problem with to-do lists is that we lose them and then start new ones. I've found that keeping mine on my computer works best. If we take it a step further and get a simple project manager program, we will really triumph in this battle. A project manager program lets us create a list of the projects we want to complete with a checklist of the steps necessary to get there. Don't get bogged down in making sure you write down each step that could possibly occur. Just add a few blank ones for the ones you cannot envision yet. Then allow yourself 50 percent more time than you think it will take.

This process has worked for me in designing book projects. At first I would feel elated that I had "finally gotten organized." Later, I would feel overwhelmed that I could never do all the tasks. Then came the feeling of being straightjacketed by the timeline. I got around this problem and still kept a reasonable schedule by putting in several little steps that I knew I could complete in less than the allotted time. When I checked those off, I was able to feel better about the whole thing and get the project done.

11. Over-Committing to Others

We often get ourselves overcommitted from a feeling of lack of love. When people ask us to do things for them we feel they won't love us if we don't. More people love us than we know and they don't base their love on what we do for them. There are also some who take advantage of us. They shove their work on us and ask us to help them do things because they are using us. We must learn to say no. The trick is to learn to say it softly but firmly. People respect us more once they realize that we value ourselves and our time.

Another time-stealer is people who ask us to run their lives for them. Frankly, since we have so much difficulty managing our own, we wonder what shape they must be in to depend on us. We have to learn to be kind to them and wean them away. This takes time, but it can be done. We could honestly tell them that we don't have time right now because we have to organize our sock drawer. They've seen our sock drawer and may believe it. After that, there is the underwear drawer, the pajama drawer and the closet. The last one is good for at least three excuses. If you have a garage, you can milk that one for six months. Everyone can identify with an untidy garage. Unless your friend is a real dunderhead, he will get the message.

12. Thinking Our Children Will Appreciate It

Hah! When was the last time your children appreciated anything? Okay, some of us may have wonderful kids, but even they are not going to be thrilled to clean out a house of garbage when we die. Believe me, because I have had to do this. The feelings that welled up in me as I sweated in the 100-degree South Texas heat were many, but appreciation was pretty far down the list.

Yes, there are some things that should be saved. Photo albums can preserve moments of our past. But double prints are probably overdoing it. Jewelry is nice to hand down to your children. Pins from every state you visited are superfluous. The ratty old moose you shot on a trip to Canada should probably be buried and given a chance to get to the happy non-hunting grounds in the sky. Clippings from the school newspaper may by enjoyed, but the whole paper, complete with lunch menus, will not. I would leave things like this for the last attack on clutter. This is a really personal area and one minefield you will have to traverse all alone. Do it only after you have some recovery under your belt. Then you will have a better eye for what to keep and what to discard.

Just imagine your children going through the stuff. You do want them to remember you with love, don't you?

4 | Getting Started

"But between the plan and the operation, there is always an unknown. That unknown spells victory or defeat....Some people call it getting the breaks. I call it God. God has His part in everything. That's where prayer comes in."

—General George S. Patton Jr.

So you've decided that you're going to tackle your mess. Hooray! It will be the hardest and most rewarding challenge you will take on. This chapter will give you an insight into the feelings that come up as you get rid of your physical mess. Chapter 7 will give you practical advice with step-by-step ways to get rid of your stuff. Don't be tempted to skip this chapter and wade right in. I've talked to those who have and they've confided that not being prepared for all the emotions that welled up sent them into a tailspin of despair. It stopped their decluttering dead in the tracks.

Immediate Gratification

By starting with the most obvious source of clutter in your life, you get immediate gratification and a feeling of success. That is the most important thing to remember. It's too easy to get bogged down with a big project. Keeping motivated may require leaving a big project and returning to one that is more manageable.

When I decluttered, I was initially filled with enthusiasm. I visualized the perfect home I would have in just a few hours. The professional organizer who visited me estimated that it would take 40 hours of her time just to make a good start. In fact, it took me months. But I did it at my pace and it was rewarding.

I started with the area around my desk. The desk was too big a project to tackle all at once. Getting the papers off the floor and the sunflower seeds (some of which were starting to sprout) out of the carpet made me feel victorious. In less than an hour I had a small area that made me feel good. I congratulated myself and stood back, surveying my realm. I was the king.

Some people start with 15 or 20 minute periods. They can commit (especially if they have a support group to fall back on) to these small periods without feeling overwhelmed. If you feel good after that period and want to keep on, go for it! For me, marathon sessions work best. Once I get into a decluttering frenzy, I go at it for hours. One Sunday I worked for nine hours. I have often spent three or four hours at a time and quit when the returns seemed to be diminishing.

I start with projects that I feel I will accomplish. I don't always succeed because they sometimes end up being bigger than I thought, but more often than not, I get them done. When it is over, I feel powerful. Pick a method of working that works for you. Do it whichever way fits your personality.

This is more than cleaning. It is an emotional roller coaster. We have this stuff because it makes us feel good or secure. When we face it again, we feel difficult emotions welling up within us. This is the time to have a decluttering partner or buddy. Your buddy doesn't have to be there; often just being available by phone is enough. (See Chapter 5 for more on the buddy system.) It just has to be someone you can call on the phone and express your emotions. It should be someone who won't belittle you for crying because you ran across movie ticket stubs from 30 years ago. Those things had meaning to you then and they still have meaning. What is hard (but necessary) is to store the memories in your brain and let many of the items go.

Mementos

Don't feel that you have to get rid of all mementos. Sure, it is best to be tough, but don't be ruthless on yourself. I held on to a lot of old letters, for instance. Great sadness came up when I reread some of them. Like the scene in *Raiders of the Lost Ark* when the Ark is finally discovered, ghosts of the past swirled around me. Lost loves, professions of undying devotion, opportunities gone forever—all floated through the room like sad wraiths.

The toughest emotions that will come up grab us when we tackle boxes with memories of relatives and friends who are no longer in this world. I was working away like a madman, having recycled more than 70 pounds of useless papers, when I hit the boxes of my mother's stuff. I uncovered every letter I had ever written her, pictures of me taking my first communion, me as a little boy, snapshots of her and my father having fun, and so on. She was such a vibrant, fun-loving woman and now she has Alzheimer's. It was like looking through a keyhole at another life and time.

I couldn't just toss those items. I had to see them and experience the emotions. I went into a trance, becoming the innocent little boy I had once been. I remembered my mother with fondness and rejoiced in the softness and warmth with which she dealt with everything in my young life. I felt sorry for all the times I had lied to her or disappointed her.

I overcame my resentment of my father. I saw for the first time that he was a human being, with fears and joys just like mine. Letters from his army days made me realize that some things never change and that we are all cut from the same cloth. Mementos of his failed businesses and the despair he experienced during financial setbacks made me see that we weren't so different.

These were all things I would have missed if I had hired someone to clean up for me. Sure, spending time on those items slowed my progress at decluttering, but they pushed me forward emotionally. I lost track of time, but when it was time to resurface to the real world, I was able to discard about 30 percent of the items and keep the ones that made the most sense to me. More importantly, I was able to file them where I could find them again. It was one of the most emotional experiences of my life and one of the most rewarding.

Shame

Shame will also come knocking. You will find things that remind you that you didn't accomplish all that you set out to do in life. Who does? I am sure that if John Kennedy or Ben Franklin looked back on their lives, they would feel regret for not having done more. Try to change that shame into mere regret. The past is gone, we cannot undo it. Don't let it rule your life. With shame-making items, you must be ruthless. Why save things that make you feel bad? I discarded rejection letters from 20 years ago. Gleefully, I thought that those nasty editors were probably dead anyway and I was finally throwing *them* into the trash. Shame was replaced by a feeling of power.

Power! Wonder! Elation!

The best emotion that will come up is power. By discarding junk from your life you are regaining the power to run your own life. Up until now, the junk was in charge. Now you are. Rejoice in it. Do a little power dance (providing you have cleared out enough stuff not to trip and fall) if you feel like it.

Wonder is another one. You will wonder why you ever kept at least one stupid thing. I had two bathtub jacuzzis that I had carted around for 15 years. At first I rejoiced that I found them. When I plugged them in and they didn't work, I wondered why I hadn't noticed that before. I gave them to Goodwill, hoping that someone would learn how to repair small motors thanks to my efforts.

Elation will come when you find items that are truly useful, which is why I don't believe in the maxim, "If you haven't used it in a year, toss it." I found old dot-matrix printer labels—10,000 of them! They are perfect file folder labels and I have used a couple of hundred of them already. I had simply forgotten that I had them, so I couldn't use them.

Once, when getting ready to go on a fishing trip, I couldn't find my surf-casting reel. This prompted me to clean out a closet where it might have been hiding. I got rid of a lot of junk there. Next, even though it was 10 p.m. and I had to leave for the airport at 5 a.m., I tackled a box that was as tall as I and had been cluttering my hallway for over a year. The reel wasn't there, and most of the stuff went into the trash, but I did find a practically new pair of leather shoes. Because

I had been wearing nothing but sneakers for several years, I thought it would be nice to dress like a grown-up once in a while. I wore those shoes to church a few weeks later.

Money Saved

You will be ecstatic at all the money you saved by decluttering. You won't have to buy half the things you thought you needed because you already have them. Just put them someplace that makes sense so you can find them when you need them.

Found Money

You will probably find cash, coins, checks, insurance policies, and so on. Consider this a bonus for having worked so hard. Enjoy that money! You earned it.

This is just a start on what it feels like to get into action. Your emotions will be your own. Feel them and then let them go, along with the clutter causing them. Your new, clutter-free life is going to be too full of future opportunities to carry around old feelings or harbor useless stuff.

5 | Clutterers' Stories

"Life (and all psychological expressions as part of life) moves ever toward overcoming, toward perfection, toward superiority, toward success. You cannot train or condition a living being for defeat."
—Alfred Adler

N early everyone has a story about some family member or friend who is a clutterer, but those stories tell the problem, not the solution. The stories in this chapter, however, are from clutterers themselves and give you a sense of how others have conquered the same problem. All are used with permission.

Samantha

Samantha has been a recovering clutterer (the term she prefers to hoarder) for nine years. She has been instrumental in the recovery of hundreds of clutterers in that time, including my own. When I first met her, I was impressed that she kept detailed to-do lists and notes. Later, I found out that this was one way she had channeled negative energy into a positive force. She used her drive and determination to keep the flame of the fledgling Clutterers Anonymous (CLA) organization from dying. To keep the meeting in North Hollywood going, she made a three-hour round trip drive every week. Always generous with her time and talents, she never said no to a request for help from a recovering clutterer.

When I interviewed her in her comfortable home, it came as no surprise that it was neat and organized. Only in part of the living room was there anything that could be construed as clutter. There were several antiques (remnants of her old business) that she was classifying and getting ready to sell. What impressed me most was her attitude. She didn't apologize or appear to feel guilty that one part of the house was less than perfect. There was a legitimate reason (not a rationalization) for the apparent disorder, and when one looked closely, one could see that the items were indeed organized. A gifted gardener, she had a patio full of beautifully planned plants and flowers. Surrounding herself with beauty is part of her recovery.

Samantha's childhood was full of anxieties. She feels she lacked healthy role models and healthy boundaries. "When I came into the program," she remembers, "I was in tremendous overwhelm. I was involved in two lawsuits and had a lot of anger. What I recognized through my years of healing was that I was more of a victim instead of a volunteer. I wasn't taking my part in my life....I had abandonment issues. I was abandoned by my mother at age two or three. I got into ACA [Adult Children of Alcoholics] and it helped. I believe that journaling is one of the greatest sources of recovery that one can do. I believe that if I feel the pain then there is the recovery....After 30 years on the antique business, I felt I had a license to collect. Now I see that the business perpetuated my collecting. I know that I have OCD tendencies....

In the beginning, I was totally out of control of my emotions. We learn to sabotage ourselves. I didn't want to deal with anything. My depression got worse to the point of apathy. We have never been acknowledged. Never been listened to. When I discovered CLA, I was home. I was listened to. My clutter buddy really helped me. The benefit of the buddy system [working with a fellow clutterer, either by telephone or in person, to help in decluttering] *was that I allowed someone to help me. Therefore I can swear by the buddy system— absolutely! Clutterers are emotional people. We react instead of act. Most of us suffer from unfulfilled expectations, unresolved guilt and childhood needs unmet.*

With cluttering, there is no one thing that causes it. I have had a tremendous amount of grief in my life.

One clutterer's trait is the desire to feel needed. Samantha used to collect clippings from newspapers and magazines to an inordinate degree. Others used her as an information source because of this. "The clippings gave me a sense of being needed," she reflects. Today, she still keeps clippings of important information, but has learned to discriminate. "I don't have to have every piece of information for others anymore," she says. Samantha believes that clutterers live with an attitude of scarcity and that buying ahead perpetuates this attitude. She feels that part of recovery is learning to live with an attitude of abundance.

Samantha has learned to differentiate between what is necessary and what is not. Her sense of self-esteem has improved so that she doesn't feel unloved just because she doesn't have the equivalent of the library reference desk. An interesting thing about this is that because of her meticulous filing and discrimination between what is important and what is not, she was able to direct me to several articles and sources for my work on this book. Had she still been stuck in her previous mindset, I wonder if she would have been able to put her fingers on the information that I needed. Samantha has taken a negative trait (storing everything) and turned it into a positive value (having important information readily and easily accessible).

When I asked Samantha what recovery felt like, or how we measure recovery, she said, "I've done ABC and I've got the whole alphabet to do. People need to learn to acknowledge themselves for what they have accomplished.... Everyone will deal with it differently. For me, it's finding one key system. Doing these things makes me have a sense of pride. I initiated the new behavior. It was easy to maintain it once it got started. Recovery freed me up to have positive energy."

Mary

I can't believe I'm writing this. No one knows about my clutter problem, except those at Clutterless meetings. I didn't have a problem with clutter in my life until my divorce. Until then, I was a little messy, often left the housework for a couple of weeks, but we lived a pretty normal life. I don't know, but after the marriage ended, I felt as if any reason to stay neat was gone too. I was in a depression and went to a therapist. She helped a lot and, I took medication for a while, which, together with the therapy, helped me over that hurdle. But we didn't talk much about my cluttering. When the depression ended, I stopped seeing my therapist, thinking the cluttering would go away too.

I kept a steady job and had to keep detailed records of phone calls. Since everything was done on a computer, this presented no problems and I used a filing system that made sense to me and to others. I was neat and presentable in my appearance and my cubicle was always clean and orderly when I left work.

But when I went home, it was like a Ms. Hyde replaced the Dr. Jekyll in my life. Newspapers piled up, on the couch at first, then the coffee table and finally [they] spilled onto the floor. I loved to read, but just didn't seem to have the time anymore.

My dishes were rinsed and put into the dishwasher at first, but for some reason, I seldom ran it. I just washed what I needed for the evening and put the rest off until 'later.' I began to retreat to bed at night and read tons of mystery novels. I began eating in bed, and somehow the dishes stayed on the floor....

The first step

I saw a notice for a Clutterers Anonymous meeting in the city where I lived at the time. Although the "anonymous" put me off (after all, I wasn't an alcoholic or drug user), I thought I would give it a try. The meetings helped me a great deal. Just finding a group of people who were like me made me feel a lot more like tackling my cluttering problem. I started decluttering and things got better. Since I didn't have a 12-step background, some of the concepts were difficult for me to grasp, but some of them did seem to apply, so I took what worked and left the rest, as they say.

Later, I went to OC [obsessive-compulsive] support groups and, while I respected them and the good they did for others, felt like I didn't fit in, since I wasn't taking medication or seeing a therapist. I certainly didn't feel like I qualified as a 'hoarder....'

I moved to a city where there was no CLA and didn't want to go back to the OC groups. Fortunately, Clutterless self-help meetings had just started and they really spoke to me. My clutter problem was not as serious as many of the people in CLA, and I didn't have a hoarding problem like those in OC groups, so, like in Goldilocks and The Three Bears, this felt 'just right.'

I had rejected religion as hypocritical when I was in college and hadn't been to a church in years. But I had read a lot of self-help books and could

identify with the general principles of what Cutterless called 'practical spiritual-
ity.' I'd never meditated, and was a little nervous about their practice of meditat-
ing during a meeting, but tried it. I was relieved that they didn't insist we get
into a lotus position (something I probably couldn't do if my life depended on it!),
or chant or anything.

"Living in lack" hit home

When the concept of 'living in lack' took root, I realized that that was what
I was doing. I thought I would never find another love and wasn't worthy, so
why bother? This was the real turning point for me. I tackled my messy house
and started to feel good about myself again. My whole personality changed. I
shed my depression as I shed my useless possessions. With the help of a buddy, I
tackled the boxes of things related to my ex and we had a big bonfire in the
backyard. God, did I feel relieved! The physical act of burning his stuff burned
him out of my consciousness.

Clutterless made me realize that my stuff wasn't my problem. I was creating
a way of life that was untrue and I had the power to change it into as good a life
as I wanted. This made sense to me. I now have a full life, a clean house, and
give dinner parties again. I found that I didn't have to have a man in my life to
feel worthwhile anymore than I had to have a lot of junk surrounding me. The
odd thing is that I now do have a man in my life, but do not feel dependent on
him, my stuff, or anyone else for my self-worth. Like they say in the meetings, true
value comes from within.

Marilyn

Marilyn has been in recovery for nine years. She is a bright, cheer-
ful person who talks about the dark days of her cluttering with humor.

She grew up in Beverly Hills, but not in a rich family. She was
surrounded by "kids who had everything" and she felt phony. Her father was ill, so her mother had to work.

I never knew anyone like me. I felt like I always had a special relationship
with God, having been a chaplain. It was so hard on me. If people only knew all
these crazy stories I had to make up to keep people who thought I was together
knowing I was not together. It makes it easy now, to just tell people I am a
clutterer. But they still only guess what a clutterer might be.

My kids say, "Mommy didn't used to be a clutterer." I've got a five bedroom house. When the kids lived there, I wasn't a clutterer. When they moved out, gradually, I filled their rooms. I'd just open a door to one of their rooms and fling something in instead of putting it away. As long as the main part of the house looked okay, I figured nobody would know. I'll take care of it tomorrow and tomorrow never came.

For me if it isn't done now, it's so easy for me to say "later" or "tomorrow." There's hardly ever "now" for me. I was so involved in EST when it was big. All the "be here now," "do this now," made me think I would change my life then. At the end, I never did think I got it. I had to take it a second time. I still wasn't sure if I got it, but I had to say I did, because I'd be too embarrassed to say that I was the only who hadn't gotten it.

If a repairman had to come to the house, I couldn't sleep the night before. I made up all kinds of crazy stories. It was all lies. I couldn't have people over to the house, I was too embarrassed. We would take our friends out to dinner instead of having them over to the house.

⟞⬦⟝

After the Northridge, California, earthquake of 1994, there was no damage to Marilyn's house, but the disarray caused by the quake was a great excuse that she used for years to justify her clutter. She had a gas oven, but wouldn't let a repairman in the house when it developed problems. A neighbor came to the front door and smelled gas. This led to a visit by the gas company. Marilyn had had a gas leak for two years.

Failure and loss

Like Samantha's story, part of Marilyn's story revolves around a business that she no longer operates and the difficulty in letting things from that go.

My cluttering was just starting then. I got in EST about the time I wanted a restaurant. I wanted that restaurant so bad. It took a year to get it together. It was my dream. I loved it. But after about a year and a half, I realized that 16 hours a day wasn't for me. I had no sense of management. People couldn't believe we closed. We always had business. Some Hollywood stars were my best customers.

After that, I was so down. I was depressed for a time. That was my dream and I couldn't make it work. I was surrounded by all the dishes that had been picked out, the antique chairs, etc. It took me so long to get it all together, the recipes all this stuff and there wasn't any of that anymore. I just couldn't get rid of them.

A crisis occurred when Marilyn's family attempted to declutter for her while she was out of town for two weeks:

My husband and daughter worked non-stop while I was gone. I wasn't grateful and had a minor nervous breakdown. They had thrown out stuff that had sentimental value, like a little blue hand my son had made as a child and a luau dress. My daughter thought the dress was tacky, but I liked it. I don't put a lot of value on monetary things. It's the sentimental value that matters. I had boxes and boxes of LA Times *food sections. Whole rooms of them. It was crazy because I made my own recipes. I didn't even miss those.*

If I'd been a part of it, I think I'd have let [the neatness] last, because in almost nothing flat, I started messing it up again. I cried a lot for two weeks. I wasn't grateful. Not being sure what a nervous breakdown was, I think I had a mini nervous breakdown.

My husband kept hoping I would be different. I would see the beauty of stuff and not the clutter. My children loved me, but they never did want to come home. I could work nonstop. There was no way to declutter it. I would put a pot with a pretty flower in it and just see the beauty and not the clutter.

My son wouldn't bring my granddaughter over for fear that she would get lost in the clutter. The phrase, 'someday it's gonna be different' was a common refrain around the house. We didn't work on this well together. I love my husband, but his way of doing something is different than mine. He is fast and I am very, very slow . And rebellious. I think he just gave up. He didn't make threats or anything else. He just gave up. He never picked up after me because I didn't want him to. I figure if I messed it up, I gotta pick it up myself.

Recovery

This conviction of Marilyn's led to her roundabout route to recovery. She started looking for Packrats Anonymous and couldn't find it. She called AA and they referred her to CLA. She recalls of her first meeting:

I just thought I was a packrat. I didn't know what a clutterer was. I'd never belonged to groups. I thought I was going to grab a handful of literature and never go back. When I heard others' stories, I realized that I was a clutterer.

My husband was happy when I got into recovery. I think he thought, 'Thank God, there's hope.' Now I don't believe he ever throws anything away without thinking 'Is this something that's going to upset her?' I think he has so much better an idea of what I am like. I don't know, it's hard to say, but I think he's turned into a little bit of a clutterer, too.

With me it's hard to work with a family member [on decluttering]. A fellow clutterer can get me to do something that a family member never in a million years can get me to do. A family member or a close friend, I don't care what they say, they will never in a million years understand a clutterer. We just don't think like other people. I don't think anyone can help me other than myself or another clutterer or turn it over to God.

Intervention didn't work for me. But maybe other people aren't as stubborn, or maybe controlling, as I was.

Time and the buddy system

I absolutely believe in the buddy system. Most of my [buddy encouragement] has worked over the phone for me.

I have kind of a thing for numbers. I want everything to total up. Certain numbers. Like threes, fives, eights. Three is for God. Five is for Jesus. Eight is a combination of God and Jesus. At a meeting we were talking about how much you can accomplish if you commit to a certain amount of time. An hour to me sounds overwhelming. Or I don't think I have an hour. So we talked about 17 minutes. I thought, good, I like 17 minutes. Seven and one adds up to eight. That equals God and Jesus.

I had a four-poster bed and each of the bedposts had a lot of clothes on them. In talking to one of the girls, said that she bet I could really declutter a post in 17 minutes. She was right. I would call her after seventeen minutes and we would decide whether to go for another 17 minutes. For me, it's too easy to get sidetracked with longer periods of time. I get overwhelmed and I overwhelm easily.

I've got to have that daily list and check things off. If I don't have a list, my memory tells me that I didn't do anything, even if I have, if I don't have a daily list, a roadmap of what I am to do that day. If I don't have that list I feel like I give myself permission to do nothing.

I liked it that God could be an even bigger part of my life with CLA. I just know that like alcoholics, they don't just go to meetings and say, "now I'm cured" and never go back. It's forever. And Clutterers Anonymous meetings are forever with me. If I didn't have 'em, I wouldn't have the constant reminders and I'd be exactly back where I was before.

Slips

I have slips all the time. While my house certainly looks better than it did when my family decluttered it...whenever anything happens that's hard to deal with, like medical bills, car repairs, or whatever, that's when I slip. I categorize clutterers as organized or disorganized clutters. I rebel against organization. If anything is going on that is hard for me to handle, like junk mail, if I don't handle right away, it fills up any empty container available. I belong to so many organizations like SPCA, Save the Whales, Save the Ladybugs, and I get so much mail that I feel I have to go through. If I am upset, I can't deal with it right away. If it isn't done now, it is so easy to say "later." Once something gets messed up, it's real hard for me to unmess it.

Richard

I came to Clutterless because my boss suggested it. It wasn't a threat, but he put it in such a way that I considered it continuing education. He had attended a few meetings and felt that it could help me. He'd spent a fortune sending me to organizing workshops, and they always seemed to help for a few weeks afterwards, but I found myself slipping into old patterns again.

I'd been a slob since childhood. I was a sloppy kid and grew up to be a sloppy adult. My mother constantly picked up after me when I lived at home. At college, I finally had to get an apartment by myself because I couldn't keep a roommate. I was a computer programmer, so I made plenty of money even then, so the extra expense didn't really bother me. I loved the cleanness and orderliness of programming. I would lose myself in that world and ignore the chaos around me.

Computer clutter

I had a really good job and plenty of money. I remained a bachelor, probably because I was an introvert. I spent most of my after work time working on my computers. I had enough money to buy a house, and just picked out some furniture. It didn't matter what the house looked like, since I lived in my computer rooms. I had six computers, several printers, and loads of other stuff like cables, motherboards, etc. Old hard drives were like molehills on my floor. I learned to walk around them. I kept getting bigger and bigger hard drives and faster processors because I would never delete files. After all, there might just be some bit of code in one of the files that I could reuse. I couldn't throw out the old computers because they might come in handy for parts. I knew this was illogical, as old technology and new technology usually don't mix, but I kept them.

Technical journals were strewn all over my home. I could never find the article I needed when I needed it, and didn't actually have time to read half of them. Sure, lots of things are on the Internet, but not always what you need.

Hitting bottom

At work, I was never neat, but I was a genius and got away with it. Then, things gradually went to pot. My company lost a huge contract because I was in charge of the development team and I lost track of our deadlines. Some of them complained that I was giving them redundant tasks and instructions that didn't make any sense. I had slipped into a fog. I was perpetually confused and spent most of my day looking for files in the jumble of my hard drive. Or just being distracted.

It all came to a head one day when I was sick and someone had to try to find some important files. They couldn't, and I couldn't explain how to find them on the phone. That's when my boss sent me to Clutterless. It felt good to know I wasn't alone. It felt better to know that I could change the self-destructive behavior. By focusing on what was right about my life, I learned that I could spill that over into the parts that were illogical. By concentrating on my success, I could create more success. By visualizing orderliness, I could bring orderliness into my life. It all made sense.

I haven't been going to meetings for long, but already I've seen improvement. Learning to break things into large subcategories and then into manageable tasks was just like writing a program. How could I have done that in programming and then forgotten to apply it to my life? But they taught me not to beat myself up for what was, and to concentrate of what is. I can make things the way I want. I had just been wanting things to be a mess.

Name Withheld by Request

—•◦—

I'm not a clutterer. I am a successful businessman. I came to Clutterless to see if there was something there to help my employees. It is practical to me to send

*them to motivational and organizing workshops and if this program had any-
thing to offer, then it was worthwhile. For some of my key employees, the workshops don't have a lasting impact, so I reasoned that an ongoing program might
be better.*

*What I saw there was practical business practices presented in a spiritual
manner. I've been a follower of Norman Vincent Peale, Tony Robbins and Og
Mandingo for years. This seems like a combination of their philosophies combined with Christ, Tao, Bhudda, New Age thought and psychotherapy. It's an
unusual mix, but it seems to work. That they invite professional people like
psychiatrists, counselors, ministers, and organizers to their meetings makes me
feel more secure than if it was just talk. Judging from the employees I've sent
there, they seem to come back with more confidence, a better attitude, and able to
clean up their messes, which were driving all of us at the office crazy.*

*I respect the anonymity factor. They are very upfront about protecting the
anonymity of those attending the meetings. Not all bosses are as understanding
as I am.*

D.T.

*I've been in therapy most of my adult life. I take SSRIs [anti-depressants].
My cluttering is an on-again, off-again problem. When the meds are working
and I am following my therapist's suggestions, my clutter problem is very small.
When I slip into depression, my stuff takes over my life. Most of the time, I look
like I live a normal life to the outside world. But when things get bad, the piles
of stuff take over.*

*OCD support groups helped me, but I like Clutterless groups too. I like the
spiritual atmosphere at Clutterless, which is different than my therapist's groups.
I like the feeling of support at both from others who won't laugh at me for my
crazy thoughts, or inability to deal with my stuff. When I am in good shape, I can
help others.*

*I don't know that I will ever be "finished" with therapy. I don't know that
I will ever get my clutter under complete control. All I know is that I feel better
after the meetings and have made some progress in cleaning out my life. They say
this goes beyond just the stuff, and I can see some of that. I feel better when I
attack the clutter, and it is a great feeling to go back to the group and tell them of
my progress. In fact, that is sometimes the only thing that spurs me on to do
something about it.*

But I don't always succeed. Sometimes I have to go and tell them that I didn't do a damn thing. They don't judge, but are supportive. This helps, and I don't feel like such a failure. I like going to meetings and think I may be getting a little better. I know I feel better.

Joe King Carrasco

Joe King Carrasco (name used with permission) is a rock-and-roll star. We don't think of people who live on the road as having a clutter problem, so his story is interesting to see how many different kinds of people cluttering affects.

Magical thinking

I don't know if it is a problem. But I have shirts from when I was 14 years old. I'm 46. I feel sometimes the stuff you touch in your life has some magical properties. I feel life is so magic. And when you find stuff, there is a magical reason. I've never thrown away any stage clothes. Some clothes seem to bring you good luck. I keep my bus from my road trips. It stopped running in 1992 or 1993. I used it for storage now. Nine bunks and each has a different item stored in it. It's kinda organized.

I drove my band crazy because I would bring six-month-old newspapers on the bus. When they realized the newspapers they were reading were six months old, they freaked. I collect cactus. Every time the bus stops on the side of the highway, I go dig up cactus. The band used to get upset, but now they are used to it, They say, "If it's not nailed down, Joe's going to take it." I save every song I've written on cassette. There are 130 tapes now. When I get to a hotel room, I throw stuff all over. People say it looks like a hand grenade went off.

I was heavy on the road in the 70s and became a Stephen C. Schlesinger fan [author of Bitter Fruit] and he wrote for The New York Times. So anywhere in the world I went I got the Times. I saved whole newspapers for 10 years. I have newspapers from my tours of Sweden and France and all over the world. I have every magazine I've ever subscribed to, notably 20 years of Texas Monthly and 10 years of Outside. Maybe I should donate them? A library?

When I lived in Austin, I kept the stuff in garbage cans. Two ladies surprised me by cleaning my apartment and threw the stuff away. I freaked out. That's when I thought I had a problem.

27 refrigerators

I've got over 27 refrigerators in my field [Joe lives in the country] since I was going to build a fence of them. Today my refrigerator is out and I don't have a working one. I have about 1,000 bottles. I bought 2,000 license plates from 1959 to 61. Paid $150. It was a deal....

I'm really big on recycling. I feel that when I am recycling and when I collect things, I am giving them a second chance. I drop all my trash in a chicken wire fence and stucco over it. I haven't thrown away any trash in 2 years, except food trash. I am trying to make it into adobe walls. I keep Fruitopia bottles to try to sell to my fans—paint 'em and put pebbles in them. Nobody wanted to buy them, so now we give them away.

You can take a stack of magazines and dip them into cement and make a brick out of it. I think everything should be recycled into walls. My new cabin has walls made out of trash. I'm into recycling but I think I have gone overboard. You know when you have 27 refrigerators you are out of touch with reality. You can't explain them to people.

I have a storage unit I rented in 1994 and I still haven't really gotten into it. You could drive a bus into it. So far I've paid $2,500 in rent. Last time I went there was a fox and black widow spiders. It was scary going in there.

Efforts to get better

I've taken efforts to clean up. I guess I am getting better, but I sure would love to come to a Clutterless meeting if there was one in Austin. I live in a one room house. It kinda keeps me under control. The more rooms you have the more stuff you can save. I solved the dishwashing problem by not having many dishes, so I have to wash them to eat. I read the newspapers on the Internet. The Internet has helped a lot. But I will always get Texas Monthly, and Outside. Forever.

All that stuff weighs you down, like anchors. It takes a whole lot of effort to get rid of stuff. In some ways I think I am eccentric. Andy Warhol was eccentric like this too. I feel sorry for whomever has to go through my shit when I die.

Name Withheld by Request

I saved this story for the last, because it is the most specific about recovery. The interviewee asked me not to reveal anything that might identify her. She is a successful businesswoman who deals with the public and is grateful for the anonymity that the programs mentioned provide. Only one paragraph about her background is included (at her request), but in my opinion, it is the most poignant.

Early life

Mother lost both parents when very young. Father was very poor. He and sibling slept on living room sofa. Mother—sloppy saver. Much stuff. Father—neat saver. Much stuff. Me—very poor when young. Carefully watched amount of food we had to eat—not enough. No movies or outside entertainment. Very few clothes. Hand-me-downs or from "cheap rack." Only one slip under dress to cover developing breasts. Washed nightly. Some nights didn't dry for school. Wore wet.

Recovery specifics

Junk mail—Battle waged for more than three years. Return it in their envelope or cut off address to tape on plain envelope, no return address. Write, "Please take off mailing list." Used to get 3.5 inches of mail per day. Now a half inch to an inch.

Magazines—Take a book to read in checkout line. Less tempted to buy magazines. Only get three magazines delivered: one news, one spiritual, one 12-step. As I read a magazine, I tear out each page read. I've learned to throw out whole unread magazines quickly. I can't be trusted to take them to a library or rest home, etc.

Bookstores—I enter no bookstores unless I have called ahead and they have my book. Buy only that book and leave.

Video stores—I enter no video stores. I for sure cannot be trusted there. I'll even end up buying a video. If I want to share video with family, read video magazine to choose, then another family member goes in alone.

Pet stores—I enter no pet stores. Used to go to "just to look," then always wanted new pet. Have three fewer pets now than when I entered CLA.

Getting rid of stuff—When you decide an object goes to the Salvation Army, put it in a dark plastic bag, never to be seen again. Wait one month before taking several full bags. The rule is if I remember an object and want it, I get it. It only happened once. I used to have two storage lockers. Now I have one. (Progress, not perfection). Each year, objects valued at $500 plus go to the Salvation Army to keep up cleaning out and get a tax credit. I've done that seven of the eight years I've been in CLA.

Bookending

I usually bookend! (Note: Bookending means calling another clutterer at the beginning of a project and then at the end of the project, or after an agreed-upon amount of time.) I need to call someone to commit that I'm starting a project now, or discuss why I'm scared to start. I call at the end or agreed-upon time. Within the last week, I called a CLA friend/buddy and said I'd start to clean out an area—a very scary area—and I'd call when I stopped. I didn't stop for almost four hours. Filled a trash barrel 2.5' diameter by 4' tall. Plus, I sorted into categories: trash, filing, craft box, scrapbook box, 12-step, other, and a box marked with a question mark [to solve later].

Commitment to meetings—I drive anywhere for a meeting. For six years I drove one and a half hours one way to get to a meeting. I've been in this program eight plus years. I go to at least one CLA meeting per week and one or two other 12-step meetings to work on the 12 steps.

The major thing I've learned: Do one thing at a time to completion or as far as you can go at the time. When interrupted, just keep returning over and over and over again, until task is complete.

6 | The Medical View

"'Compulsive' and 'obsessive' have become everyday words....This is not how these words are used to describe Obsessive-Compulsive Disorder (OCD), a strange and fascinating sickness of ritual and doubts run wild.

—Judith L. Rapoport, M.D.,
The Boy Who Couldn't Stop Washing

Although most readers of this book probably have not been diagnosed as hoarders, or as Obsessive-Compulsive personalities, the difference, in my opinion, is one of degree. Many of us may well benefit from psychotherapy and would like to know what is available according to experts in the field. If your cluttering seems beyond your control, then please consider the opinions of the experts presented in this chapter. I hope that many in the helping professions will be reading this book and will find it useful to have a distillation of the current opinions and research in one handy place, as presented here. I have refrained from editorializing or commenting on the views of the medical and psychological experts whom I interviewed for this chapter. We probably all know someone with OCD characteristics, and this chapter should be valuable to everyone who wants to know more about this fairly common and widely misunderstood condition.

Definitions

The medically recognized term for the disorder is "hoarding." Hoarding is an Obsessive Compulsive Disorder, classified in the *Diagnostic and Statistical Manual of Mental Disorders* (fourth edition) as diagnosis 300.3. Obsessive Compulsive Personality Disorder, a different condition, is diagnosis 301.4. The general consensus is that OCD is caused (or exacerbated) by a chemical misfire in the brain relating to serotonin levels.

The *DSM-IV* (as it is abbreviated) defines an obsession as "persistent thoughts, impulses, or images expressed as intrusive and inappropriate and that cause marked anxiety or distress." A compulsion is, "repetitive behavior (checking, counting, etc.), or mental acts, the goal of which is to prevent or reduce anxiety or distress."

Hoarding is a medical diagnosis. Cluttering is a layman's term. John P. Zak, M.D., associate professor and director of clinical services at the University of South Florida's Dept. of Psychiatry, gave me this distinction. "The definitions of 'hoarding' and 'cluttering' are not clear; especially comparatively speaking. Probably clutterers can purge or 'excavate' the clutter with little or no anxiety/irritability involved. A hoarder finds it very difficult to get rid of the stuff without the occurrence of severe distress unless it is done in a very systematic, well planned out, therapeutic approach."

Dr. Randy Frost, another of the authorities on hoarding and author of several papers and books on the subject, defined compulsive hoarding as "the acquisition of and failure to discard possessions which appear to be useless or of limited value."

[Note: There is a medical condition called "cluttering," but it is related to stuttering. If you do a Web search on "clutter" it will frequently come up, as will Web sites selling organizing tools.]

Obsessive-Compulsive Disorder

"My doctor said I had OCD. I couldn't believe it.
I had to call him nine times to make sure."

—Judy Gold, *comedian*

There are several criteria that must be met to qualify a behavior as a case of OCD: The action (in this case, hoarding) must cause marked distress, be time-consuming (occupying more than an hour a day), or significantly interfere with one's occupational functioning or usual social routines.

Dr. Gail Steketee is one of the nation's leading experts on hoarding. She is professor and chair of the clinical practice department at the Boston University School of Social Work. She has more than 20 years of research experience and is the author of: *When Once is Not Enough: Treatment for Obsessive Compulsive Disorder* and *Overcoming Obsessive Compulsive Disorder: Behavioral and Cognitive Therapy.* She and Teresa Pigott, M.D., were co-editors of what I think is the best primer on OCD for the layperson: *Obsessive Compulsive Disorder, The Latest Assessment and Treatment Strategies.*

According to Dr. Steketee, "OCD is anxiety-based fear. Saving is compulsive. Impulsive alcoholics and overeaters have a drive to do something and overdo it. They want to eat because it is pleasurable. In many cases, this applies to the acquisition aspect of hoarding. Many people buy things they want even though don't have a place for them. They have an appetite for it. It is not fear-related."

The average age of OCD onset is the mid 20s to early 30s. Many people lead fairly normal lives despite their hoarding/cluttering, but the problem usually escalates as they get older. Note that obsessive-compulsive disorders can be associated with major depressive disorder or other anxiety disorders, such as specific phobias, social phobia, panic disorders, eating disorders, and OCPD (obsessive-compulsive personality disorder).

As noted earlier, OCPD is its own condition. Some of its symptoms are a rigid personality, the inability delegate, a belief that no one else can do things right, stinginess or sense of lack, and an inability to prioritize. People with OCPD express affection in a highly stilted or controlled manner. They are preoccupied with logic and lack flexibility and the ability to compromise. There is a correlation between OCPD and mood or anxiety disorders. OCPD is two times as likely to appear in men, according to the *DSM-IV*.

Prevalence of OCD and Hoarding

One in 40 Americans, or 6.5 million people, suffer from this disorder, making it one of the most common mental disorders. OCD is equally likely to appear in men as women. While many OCD symptoms manifest themselves in children, hoarding seems to onset in adolescence and early adulthood. Dr. Steketee told me that one-fourth to one-third of people with OCD are hoarders. My research indicated that self-diagnosed cluttering (remember, this is not a medical term) is more common. Most people I talked to think they have a cluttering problem, or know someone who does. These are not people who are living in squalor, or who are imprisoned by uncontrollable obsessions. They are normal people who just don't know what to do with all their stuff. I have noticed in my anecdotal research that hoarders or clutterers seem to have problems with their memories. Dr. Steketee suggested that the "main problem is confidence in memory."

Just because you clutter doesn't mean that you have OCD. Most perfectly functioning people have some rituals, according to Obsessive-Compulsive Foundation literature, *Learning to Live With OCD*. The OC Foundation is the first place to go for easy-to-understand literature on these disorders. For more information on the foundation's work and the books and pamphlets available, call 203-878-5669 or write to The OC Foundation, P.O. Box 70, Milford, CT 06460.

Therapy and Medication

Psychiatrists and psychologists said that professional help should be considered if the symptoms are severe and are causing a lot of distress in a person's personal or professional life. People with OCD usually resist therapy and tend not to be rational about their disorder. The general consensus in the medical community is that a combination of therapy and medication is preferred.

I asked John P. Zak, M.D., associate professor and director of clinical services in the department of psychiatry at the University of South Florida for his opinion on the subject. He believes "There is no one answer for the question as to whether medication alone, medication in conjunction with therapy, or therapy alone is the approach for treatment. This must be uniquely individualized for each patient. Some patients are unable or unwilling to engage in both forms of treatment and therefore we must work with the alternative form of treatment. Some patients cannot engage in the behavioral treatment due to the intensity of their symptoms interfering with the necessary process. However, if they respond at least somewhat favorably to medication, they may then become more able to engage in the behavior therapy process." Nada L. Stotland, M.D., M.P.H., a professor of psychiatry at Rush Medical College, told me that many psychiatrists "would probably start with medication plus psychotherapy. Medication alone is probably not sufficient for most patients. Psychotherapy alone may work for some. Combination treatment is best."

Recovery Rates

Although I read a study that claimed that 76 percent of hoarders improve with cognitive-behavioral therapy, Dr. Steketee said that there is "nowhere near enough experience" to determine this for sure. The study I read had very few subjects. "There is a need for follow-up," she says. "More than half of those in therapy benefited in only a few months. Length of treatment is the biggest challenge." Dr. Stotland agrees. "I doubt there are really good data on this; there are so many hoarders that don't come to clinical attention," she notes.

May Not Be OCD

Dr. Steketee acknowledges that hoarding may not really belong in the OCD category "Hoarding may not really reflect OCD-like symptoms," she says. "We are in limbo for diagnostic understanding. It is not clear where hoarding belongs. Hoarding has a different basis for different individuals. For some, it is fear-based. For some [it is] not wasting. It is far more important to understand why symptoms develop and are maintained."

A Knotty Problem

Jean Goodwin, a Galveston, Texas, psychiatrist, calls hoarding "a knotty problem." She notes that psychodynamic treatment approaches (those based on the theories of Freud and his followers) are still useful, but are often combined with behavioral or cognitive therapies. In psychodynamic therapy, the emphasis is on the patient's relationships with others and on a wide-ranging exploration of the psyche. In cognitive-behavioral therapy, specific coping and motivational strategies are emphasized. Goodwin believes that hoarding may be intertwined with other issues, such as low self-esteem, passivity, hesitation, and self-doubt.

"Cleaning is a common OCD symptom. Paradoxically, messiness or not cleaning can be a way to cope with the same set of obsessions," Goodwin says. Drug therapy is sometimes indicated. Because the medications take about three months to reach their maximum effectiveness, there must be "a good deal of commitment," on the part of the patient, Goodwin says.

Art Therapy

Catherine Deyo, a counselor at Galveston Counseling and Mediation Services, is an art therapist. She has found that working with different media helps people with OCD to get out of their trapped thinking. She likes to "playfully encourage" a change from resistive media, like mosaics, to something more fluid to open up their channels of creativity. "I encourage OCD people to play...to get out of their heads and feel." She says a common OCD statement is "I didn't get to be a kid." There is a lack of balance in the lives of people with OCD, she says. They are generally serious. "My goal is to make them feel more comfortable," says Deyo. Through her work, she seeks to teach tolerance.

As Deyo sees it, people with OCD suffer from "security overwhelm." They develop "magical thinking," and hope that "objects can create control [and] safety." They do not realize they are doing this. Deyo also emphasizes cognitive-behavioral therapy, because, she says, as children, people with OCD didn't have the resources to cope with things. She strives to give them those resources as adults. "If the patient is motivated, he can revisit earlier times with his adult resources, gain understanding, and put them aside," she says. Once again, this takes commitment on the patient's part, as it cannot be done in a brief period of time. However, "OCD people avoid therapy," Deyo notes. She emphasizes that "handling [OCD issues] head-on without behavioral therapy is not effective."

Dr. Zak believes that "It is possible that a hoarder can completely recover without ongoing therapy. It is probably dependent on the quality of the therapy initially and the personality structure of the individual hoarder. We must keep in mind that there is no absolute point at which we can determine what is hoarding and what is not. If there is absolutely no saving or collecting behaviors, we can state there is complete recovery, but if there is any of those behaviors, the perception of recovery lies within the individual—for example, if the person feels comfortable and experiences no dysfunction due to the minimal behavior."

Anxiety

One medical definition of anxiety is "a feeling of apprehension with no obvious, immediate cause." A hoarder with such anxiety holds onto his possessions for no real reason. However, he may well have rationalizations for his behavior, such as, "It will come in handy someday," "These things cost good money; it would be a sin to waste them," and, "I was taught to 'waste not, want not.'"

Anxiety is not fear. Fear is a reaction to a definite threat. New York psychiatrist Dr. Anthony Cozzolino explained it to me as follows: A soldier in battle has fear—fear of loss of life, fear of not performing well. When you are attacked by a mugger, your fear is real and has a definite form. You fear losing your possessions or your life. When the mugger goes away, the fear is gone. Someone with an anxiety disorder will believe that every stranger from that point on is a potential mugger.

Anxiety is indefinite, vague. People with anxiety worry that the fabric that holds their world together will be rent. Sometimes, anxiety is normal. Anxiety precedes growth. We all have anxiety when we change or grow. A normal person experiences anxiety when he begins a new job, or moves to a new house. Someone with neurotic anxiety believes the job will be terrible, and he will fail and be fired. He worries that the house will have hidden structural defects, the neighborhood will go to pot, or a gang will move in next door.

Obsessions

The obsession of a hoarder to hoard things (whatever the reason) causes anxiety. He feels compelled to relieve the pain of the anxiety, but doesn't have the tools to do so. His behavior is not conscious. A hoarder's feeling of lack of control over his life—anxiety—results in his exerting control over his possessions. The irony of this is that the possessions end up causing more anxiety in his home life, paralyzing him.

Therapy and Self-Help Groups

Marsha Davidson, a therapist in Orange County, California, has more than 30 years of experience in, as she puts it, "communication skills." She believes that self-help or 12-step groups can provide the support systems people in crisis need. One problem in entering therapy is that you are "coming out of the closet," and a support group can help alleviate the feeling of being unique or isolated.

Anthony Cozzolino offers this observation: "People who already attend 12-step programs already have some self-awareness and are likely to seek help. The majority of OCD sufferers do not have this self-awareness and do not seek help on their own."

Exposure Rituals

Psychiatrists often use a method called exposure rituals with OCD patients to get them to face their fear through a visualization or tape. For hoarders, such a ritual might be to imagine that they have thrown everything away and imagine the worst consequences. Then, when these dire consequences are proven impossible, or at least highly unlikely, the hoarder may be able to move on to really eliminating the stuff.

According to Steven Phillipson, Ph.D., staff psychologist at the Institute for Behavior Therapy, New York City, "The primary objective of cognitive-behavior therapy for OCD is to starve the demon of its nourishment (that is, avoid any thoughts or behaviors that are reassuring, avoidant or escapist in nature). Impatience for the anxiety to go away is the demon's greatest ally. Choosing to embark on the long path of eliminating this disorder requires realizing that the goal of starving an enemy to death takes time."

If you decide to seek professional help for your hoarding, ask your psychotherapist or psychiatrist if he or she specializes in hoarding, or at least in OCD.

Community Health Issues

Dr. Stotland notes that cluttering can significantly affect the community at large, "particularly [in cases of] psychotic patients, who may be kicked out of their housing because of all the clutter. They are not necessarily hoarding particular things." Also, community health officials are often called when someone's hoarding causes a significant odor, or when abandoned appliances and junk cars pose a danger to children in the community.

Sometimes, when the police are called in on domestic disputes, they see a situation of hoarding that requires social services to come out. There have been cases of families losing their children because of the unsanitary conditions.

I personally counseled a hoarder whose cluttering had brought him to the attention of the police. It started with shopping carts. He had two dozen behind his apartment. This led to the manager's knocking on his door. When she saw the clutter inside, she threatened to evict him. They got into a brawl. The shopping cart dilemma was easy to fix; there are services in large cities that collect the carts for stores. (The stores are happy to get them back and rarely prosecute the hoarder. If you have a stash of shopping carts, call a store manager and he will tell you what to do.) The assault charges and the eviction were more difficult to resolve. The man entered counseling and eventually got into recovery.

More Research Needed

Everyone I talked to in the medical community agrees that more research needs to be done on the causes and treatments of OCD in general and hoarding in particular. Even if drug therapy is effective, unless the behavioral aspects of the disorder are treated, patients return to old behaviors very quickly once they discontinue their medication.

7 | A Clutter Diary

"We can conquer only by attacking."
—General George S. Patton Jr.

9:22 p.m.

I can't put it off any longer. I've eaten dinner, washed the dishes (a great way to put off more distasteful tasks, yet feel good about yourself), watched TV (you think you have problems—Captain Kirk just lost his warp drive) and made fresh espresso (grinding takes longer). I've felt every cigar in my humidor and found the one that is closest to perfection (that took a good 10 minutes).

9:30 p.m.

It turns out I could put it off longer. I had to decide which of the two most distasteful tasks to do—balancing my checkbook (for the first time in well, forever), or emptying the box that might have some bank statements in it. I start with the box. Now, do I file the things in it, or just rummage through the stuff to find the bank statements? I elect to do a clean, honest job of decluttering. I file away.

Found my Social Security statement of earnings for the last 10 years. And here's an article that is crucial to this book. Guess I'd better get a file folder for that. Fortunately, as a result of some hard-won organization, I know exactly where the file folders *and* the labels are. They are right where they belong. Good. I have made some progress. I made a home for like things when I moved and have kept the promise of using it. That one little victory gives me a great feeling of accomplishment. It spurs me on.

I haven't called my clutter buddy yet. I'm not that scared. I can do this on my own.

10:05 p.m.

Okay, I *am* that scared. Scared of what? I think scared of finding how much more I have to do. I have been slipping since the move from L.A. More junk came in and I did not deal with it. I unpacked most of my stuff and discarded much of it but got to a point of comfort and quit. Making a living and trying to have a life got in the way. Now I am blocked, emotionally and financially. Suze Orman talks about clearing out the clutter to get your financial affairs rolling. Smart woman, that Suze.

I call my clutter buddy to tell her I am starting. She is not there, but just leaving a message on her machine is enough. It makes me commit. Now I have to really start.

10:15 p.m.

I really need some music. I have found that when decluttering, classical music (much as I love it) doesn't work. Rock, Bob Dylan, Ricky Nelson, Joe King Carrasco and Big Band work better for me. Joe King really gets the adrenaline flowing. Now I'm nearly at the end of the box. Haven't found a bank statement, but did find some valuable paperwork I thought I'd lost.

10:30 p.m.

Found 60 colones (Costa Rican dollars) from a trip to Costa Rica. Now that's going to come in handy! Put them aside to give to some kid. I've done this before and really did give it to a kid. That is progress. Found pictures (it is usually a mistake to sort pictures when decluttering, but I am on a roll and feel nothing can stop me). Threw 80 percent of the first two stacks away. Some dated back to the days when I lived in

Mexico and had a 22″ waist and a Swedish girlfriend. Those are price-less and are filed away under "Memories." I have been ruthless with my memories and have kept nearly 50 years of them in two banker's boxes. I kept my baby pictures, trashed the rejection letters from editors. That part I enjoyed.

Pictures bring back memories, which can usually slow a decluttering job. I must be getting better, because these didn't. I did reflect that I once lived in a one-room house, slept on a cot, and could fit everything I owned and needed into a duffel bag—including my tiny electronic typewriter. I banged out my first unpublished novel on that little ma-chine. I gave it to charity 15 years later, when I was in Los Angeles. It was hard to part with.

11 p.m.

When I get to the third set of pictures, I stop looking through them and stuff them into a "pictures to be sorted" box. Sorting photos is a low priority, time-consuming job without big visible rewards, and as such is best done on a rainy day in front of the TV.

Found several disks for computer programs. They used to be hard to get rid of. This stems from the feeling of lack I had when I lived in an attic in Seattle, with not much more than a duffel bag and a computer. As an unsuccessful writer with no job and a lot of hope, I didn't have a lot of disks. Now I would have thousands if I didn't discard them. Know-ing where the feelings come from is good. It helps us realize that we are not in that space anymore and that our need to hold on to some things (well, probably most things, but we deal with each item separately) is irrational. We are not the people we were 20 years ago.

Threw disks into a box for Goodwill. They are good programs and maybe someone less fortunate than I can use them. Maybe they will find their way into the hands of a struggling writer.

11:15 p.m.

Finished the box. Discarded about 60 percent of the contents over-all. Found two contracts for my business and the instructions to some of my computer hardware that I needed weeks ago. Filed the important things. Hit a small box and made short work of it. Now have two square feet of floor space. It feels good. Still feeling full of pep, so attack a shelf with unread mail.

11:35 p.m.

Called my clutter buddy to let her know that I was still at it. We chatted for a while. It made me feel better and even more enthusiastic about my progress. While talking to her, found another month's bank statement!

11:45 p.m.

Wow! Found a 1099 from a publisher in the unread mail. Kind of sad that I only made $3,000 from that book last year, but at least I know. Many of us are so disorganized that we fear doing our taxes, sometimes putting it off for years. All the while, that fear is creating mental clutter and paralyzing us in other aspects of our lives. Found another piece of tax info.

12:05 p.m.

Called a girlfriend to share my excitement, "I'm decluttering and writing in my clutter journal!" Without meaning to, she deflated me with the statement, "Is this day one?" "You don't know where I came from," I replied, hurt. This is a problem that we clutterers have to face. Others do not always understand how hard it is for us to climb out of the boxes we have created for ourselves. Family members can be a tremendous source of support, and we need and appreciate that. But, no matter how far we have come, we are still emotionally raw. We cannot and do not expect others to tiptoe around us. Part of recovery is learning how to be resilient in the face of imagined slights. And they are mostly imagined. Real recovery would probably be not imagining the slights at all, but I ain't there yet. We are such sensitive people that we magnify every non-supportive word into a cascading Niagara of criticism. This is not just a problem of too much stuff. It is a disease of guilt, shame, and poor self-image.

It's foolish, I know, but now I feel like the thousands of pounds of junk that I discarded, the progress from using a 24-foot moving van to a 15-foot one and the making of homes for stuff in my new house all count for nothing. I wallow in self-pity and want to quit. I half expect some jack-booted officer from the "normal patrol" to burst into my house and shout, "Just get over it, you whiner." But right now I feel, "What's the use?"

After writing this, and making it clear to myself, I am ready to get back at it. Writing our feelings out is good, cheap therapy. But my enthusiasm is waning. I am now just going through the motions. Lesson: be careful whom you share your decluttering successes with. Sometimes our mountains of progress are molehills of dung to normal people. And there are more of them than us.

1:45 a.m.

Calling it quits. Didn't get checking account balanced, but have more material than before. Found a check for $32.84 and two book orders for another $43.90. Suze Orman was right. The prosperity is flowing in already. Cleared some more space. Read and disposed of all the mail. Now have clear space on shelf. Moved a small bookshelf to a better location, clearing a walkway. Should feel really good about what I got done, but just down from the one negative comment. Damn, I wish I wasn't like this. To be normal, to be normal.

8 | Practical Steps to Eliminate Clutter

"Never wear anything that panics the cat."
—P.J. O'Rourke

O kay, now that you have decided that you want a new way of life, let's get off our cerebrums, roll up our sleeves, and dig in! While I touched upon making choices of how to declutter in Chapter 4, they were from a very personal point of view. This chapter is more detached.

When you declutter for the first time, you may be so ashamed about your mess that you do not want anyone to help you, or you may be so overwhelmed that you need someone to help you get started. There is no right way. Attack the problem whichever way seems to work best for you. And, if you find that it isn't working, change tactics.

If you want to have someone help you, whom do you choose? A professional organizer? A friend? Relative? Fellow clutterer? There are pros and cons to each. They are listed in my personal order of preference.

Doing It Yourself

Pros

You work at your own pace. There is little shame (though from time to time you may beat yourself up for getting into this mess). It is free (financially anyway—you have already paid a high emotional price). You decide what is important and what is not. You get a tremendous sense of accomplishment with every little step. You can step back and admire your work as frequently as you like. You can cry unabashedly when your emotions overwhelm you.

Cons

You may not be able to even start. You may feel overwhelmed from the beginning. You may not be able to decide where to begin. You may get stuck. You may get overwhelmed in the middle of the project. You may become so depressed that you can't go on. You may feel like you have made real progress when, in fact, you have hardly begun. You may never get finished.

Other Clutterers

Pros

This is the best choice if you are going to ask for help. They understand. They will go at your pace, taking time out to comfort you when the emotions get overwhelming. They will be flexible in deciding where things should go and understand when you just can't let go of something. By the same token, since they have been there, they will not let you get away with doing nothing. You had better express your thanks by taking them out to a nice dinner, buying them a massage, or offering to help them work on their own clutter.

Cons

They might be too sensitive to your needs and not press you to make some tough decisions. It may take longer, as you will engage in conversations about why things area the way they are. They, too, may become overwhelmed and quit in the middle of the job.

Friends

Pros

If you have friends who have actually been to your home and remain friends, they have a lot going for them. They like you anyway. You don't have to pay them, though you should at least take them out to a nice dinner or two to express your gratitude. They have wanted to help you for however long you have known them and they appreciate being asked. They will have the very best of intentions.

Cons

It could wreck your friendship. Even though they may love you, they will not really understand why you have so much stuff, nor why you are attached to, say, your collection of paper sacks. If they are take-charge kind of people, they may (in your sensitive opinion) bully you into doing things you don't want to do. That can build resentments. Being a good clutterer, you love to hold onto resentments. At some point they may become exasperated with you. They may give up in the middle of the project because they cannot deal with the mess and the emotions.

Professional Organizers

Pros

These people have seen it all. They will not judge you. You will be paying them to do a job and they are not emotionally involved. You can go away and they will do the whole thing for you.

Cons

They are expensive ($35 to $125 an hour). My own experience was that I was given quotes ranging from $500 for a one bedroom apartment to $2,000 for a two bedroom apartment. They operate on set principles of how things should work, which may not work for you. Some of them can be tough. Although most are understanding people, it is inevitable that they will discard things that make no sense to them, yet may be really valuable to you.

How to do it

You have already taken the first step by choosing the method you are going to use. Most people will choose to do it themselves, at least at first. The principles here will apply to all methods except the professional organizer route. (They have their own way of doing things and many not like it if you suggest doing it your way.) We are only going to deal with your temple, your house, not your garage or storage areas. First things first. Get your house in order and the rest will follow.

1. Prepare physically

The day before you begin, buy a huge supply of trash bags (the really big, heavy-duty ones), banker's boxes (cardboard boxes of a uniform size used for filing, found in any office supply store), several felt tip pens (you will lose some in the decluttering), file folders, hanging files, lots of coffee, soda, tea, or whatever you drink (decluttering is thirsty work), some snack food (unless you are an overeater), and pre-cooked lunches and dinners (you don't want to take time out for cooking and lose your momentum). Find your CDs or tapes and your portable player and have them in one place so you won't have to hunt for them. Rock and roll seems to work best for me, though a classical break comes in handy when the stress level gets intolerable. Avoid soothing sounds. You need to get that adrenaline pumping.

Take a picture of every room in your house. Take wide shots and close-ups. Take them to a one-hour developing place while you shop for your decluttering arsenal. When you get home, the very first thing you should do is to file the pictures away where you will be able to find them. If you use a Polaroid, file them immediately. You will need these to give yourself moral support when you have a slip. Take pictures of each room or area as you get it into order. File these pictures alongside the ones of your original mess. Look at them whenever you get into a funk.

Get a good night's sleep. You will need all your emotional and physical energy for the task ahead.

On D-Day (declutter day) get up early. An early start seems to help. Visualize yourself as General Patton and declare that you are going to go through your clutter "like crap through a goose." Wear old clothes, as it is often dirty work. If it helps, wear combat fatigues to enhance the battle metaphor. A flack jacket or helmet is probably overdoing it.

2. Prepare emotionally and spiritually

Before you begin, meditate. (If you are using a partner, it would be nice for them to do so too, but it's not necessary. It is your emotions that need to be in order.) If you don't meditate already, don't worry. You do not have to twist yourself into a lotus position and chant "ooommm." Sit or lie down. I mediate during my morning bath, preparing myself with a cup of espresso and a cigar. It works for me. Some people use mood music, soothing sounds of water or forests, or classical music to help them get into the right state of mind. Others find this distracting. Pick the music that fits you.

Put yourself into a calm, relaxed state by breathing deeply with your eyes closed. When you are sufficiently relaxed, visualize yourself going through your house and decluttering perfectly, joyfully, peacefully. See what your home will look like when you are finished. Feel the perfect peace and joy that will be yours when your house looks like this. See yourself inviting friends over for a party to celebrate your success. Feel the pride you have as you show them room after room of a graceful environment. Enjoy those feelings of pride and contentment for as long as you want. Make them feel real. When you are ready, gradually come back to this plane.

You will find yourself calm and full of energy. You may find that as you work, you start to get stressed out and anxious again. Feel free to take a meditation break.

3. Begin with something that will give you immediate gratification

Forget beginning with a drawer. It is hidden and you will not be able to look back on it with pride. Your bed is probably cluttered with books, clothes, dishes from late night ice-cream binges (well, mine was) and God knows what else. Wouldn't it be nice to actually be able to slide into bed without having to wedge yourself in between the debris? Many have a tendency to surround ourselves with possessions so that we will feel secure in our rest.

Perhaps you'd like to start with your desk. If you work at home, think of how much more efficient you will be when you have a clean space to work! Leave the file drawers for last.

Maybe you want to begin with your front room. If you have to give visitors a map to find the pathways from the door to the sofa, imagine your pride when you can just open the door and say, "Come right in. Have a seat on the sofa."

Whatever you choose, start with a manageable part. Some people go best starting with a 15 or 20 minute period devoted to decluttering. If that seems manageable to you, then by all means do it. Personally, I like to start with a goal of getting a specific area or room done. Whatever works for you is the way to go. If one way doesn't work, try another. If you need to develop your own way, do it. Just do it!

Don't get bogged down with organizing where things will go. I know that the professional organizers are big on this, but clutterers often use this as an excuse to avoid doing any real work. Just dig in. The organizing part will follow.

4. D-Day—Storm the bastions of clutter!

You will need a staging area, a place to put stuff. Just shovel a bunch of stuff from one corner of the room to clear a space. Try to put things you are going to keep into piles of "like things." Don't overcomplicate this. All music stuff is "like." All outdoors stuff is "like." Don't take the time now to sub-categorize it into camping, fishing, mountain-climbing, parachuting, etc. That can come later.

Papers are the hardest. It is best to have a filing cabinet ready and to put them into hanging folders with general tabs, like "important papers," where you will put your mortgage, marriage/divorce papers, birth/death certificates, tax stuff, etc. Don't get bogged down with making individual files. You can do that later.

You may want to start with your bedroom and make it your sanctuary. The drawback to this is that it may be the toughest challenge and you could get bogged down or depressed. It helps to remember that it is where you will probably meditate and nourish your spirit. The bathroom is usually the easiest and fastest and may jump-start you to tackling bigger projects. The kitchen should come next, as you go there everyday and prepare nourishment for your body. The dining room should be next, as it is where you will bring the fruits of your kitchen labors. The living room is best left for last, as you probably don't do a lot of entertaining in it.

The Bedroom

Clothing

The best way to help you decide how many of what to keep is to remember that you are probably never too far from a washing machine. So, how long do you want to go between washes? I keep enough clothes to get me through eight days. That's a week between washes with a day for procrastination.

If you start with clothing, you can put the small stuff (underwear, socks, and the like) into banker's boxes. Label them. Larger items (dresses, shirts, pants, and so on) need a large cardboard box. Don't just throw them into a pile. You will never get rid of the pile. Don't start hanging things up just yet. That requires some thought, and too much thinking at this stage could slow you down. If you do actually start with a closet, the goal is to empty it enough to know what you have and find it.

If you wear a garment, put it into the clothing "keeper" pile. If you don't wear it anymore, make a pile for charitable donations. If you are honest with yourself throughout this process, the charity pile will probably be larger than the keeper pile. If you already have drawers with space available, go ahead and put socks in the sock drawer, undies in the undies drawer, and so on. Chances are, you will have too many of each. Now we're cooking.

Socks and stockings

How many socks do you need? I opt for seven to 10 pair. Put the ones with sagging elastic, missing partners, and holes into a rag bag or throw them out. Goodwill doesn't want them. Toss 'em.

I helped declutter a friend who had more than 100 pairs of socks, many never worn. She bought new ones because she couldn't find the ones she had. She had a real emotional attachment to them and it was difficult for her to cut down to a (in my opinion) reasonable number.

We finally compromised and she put most of them into a garbage bag with the stipulation that she would not open it for a month. If a month passed and she saw that she didn't need them, she agreed to throw them away. It did and she did. Sometimes stopgap measures are necessary.

Pantyhose are cheap and run easily. Chuck the ones with runs. The same is true for real hose. Garter belts always seem to lose one of the snaps. (Hey, I used to be a traveling lingerie salesman, so don't get any ideas). Don't bother Goodwill with them. Out they go.

Shirts, pants, and dresses

You will find some hardly worn items in this category. They were lovely on the shelf and might have looked lovely on you once. But now they don't fit or they are out of style. Don't let feelings of shame about how you have filled out bog you down. Keep about one-fifth of the ones that don't fit now in case you can ever wear them again. I did, and guess what—I actually lost weight when I shed those extra pounds of clutter! It could happen. If it doesn't, you can always throw them away at a later date. By getting rid of the ones that are frayed, way out of style, or just plain ugly, you will feel good and not deprived.

Shoes

I had 18 pairs of shoes and boots. Some of them had hardly been worn. Many other clutterers I have helped have had numbers ranging in the hundreds. How we dealt with them: The ones that need fixing should go. Period. The ones that are too small should go. Period. Even if you lose weight, your feet are will not shrink significantly. That will take care of half of them.

Specialty shoes or boots deserve a chance. I kept one pair of hiking shoes, one pair of hiking boots, a pair of winter boots (I travel a lot), three pairs of sneakers that were in good shape, and two pairs of leather shoes (which I only wear when I have to). That's eight pair. The rest went. Women will have ones that only go with certain dresses. Keep them if you still have the dress and you can fit into it. Otherwise, toss 'em.

Coats and jackets

There is nothing wrong with having more than one winter coat. A dozen may be too many. Try to get somewhere in between. A ski jacket, a leather jacket, a car coat, a dress cashmere coat, and a ratty old coat that you use when fishing or shoveling snow should about cover it. This is one area where you can really be a hero. There are plenty of homeless and poor people who will appreciate any coat that is warm, even if it does have some holes in it. Give yours away and feel very, very good about yourself.

Suit jackets are a little tougher. Yes, they cost way too much to begin with. Yes, they looked good once. But think about it. Can you go to your next meeting wearing a suit that went out of fashion when the Bee Gees were making hits? If they don't fit well, don't look good, or aren't perfect, throw them out.

Pants, shirts, dresses

See the above paragraph. What you wear says a lot about you. What are your clothes saying about you?

T-shirts

Like socks, these proliferate like rabbits. And, thanks to those simpleminded friends who can't bring us real gifts from their globe-trotting, we are always getting more. Be ruthless here. My daily dress consists of a tee shirt and a pair of shorts, socks and sneakers, since I live on the beach. I have seven tees and five shorts. My "dress" tees (those not advertising somewhere) are another story. I consider them a different category. I have five of those.

Hats

Hats are like shoes. Keep one for each occasion, but be honest about how many occasions there are.

Other items of clothing

If you surf or dive, you probably have a wet suit. But if you have expanded and it hasn't, it's useless. Sell it. With anything else that you uncover, ask, "Do I really use this anymore?" Be honest.

The Kitchen

One of the greatest joys in my clutter-free life is walking into a clean kitchen. As decluttering goes, this is one of the easier areas to keep clean.

Dishes

You will probably have to wash most of them. To do that, you'll probably have to get the piles of algae and e-coli breeding grounds out of the sink so you can scour it. Rubber gloves are a good idea. You won't have a place to put the dishes you're about to wash without putting away the few you have already washed, and doing something with the piles of newspaper and whatever else clutters your kitchen counters. Don't get distracted. Shovel all the junk on the counters into bags and go through them later. The goal here is to create space for the dishes you have. Pots and pans take up a lot of real estate. Put them on the stove.

The sink probably needs scouring powder and bleach (used separately) to disinfect it. After you scrub it, soak it in bleach. While that is happening, sweep the floor. By the time you've finished sweeping, the sink will be safe. Dump the moldy dishes in it and soak them in bleach. While they soak, scrub the counter.

This is a good time to go through the shelves and discard the dishes that are clean (except for the dust they have collected from years of not being used). Pitch 'em.

Sure there is some emotion here, particularly if the dishes were given to you by a favorite aunt or inherited from your parents. If there are complete (or nearly so) sets of china or "good dishes," and you have room for them, put them all together. If you don't, put them in sturdy boxes, label them, and get them out of the kitchen. If you have an inordinate amount of real silverware, please don't get your hopes up that it is worth a fortune. I helped a clutterer cart several pounds of silverware to a dealer and she got very little. If it is a rare set, it is a different story. I wish you the best, but don't want to get your hopes up.

Now to the everyday dishes. You have two choices—you can wash everything and then decide what to discard, or you can save yourself a step. I prefer throwing the cracked plates, glasses, and bowls into the trash while they're still dirty. I get a thrill out of smashing them. It makes me feel like I am smashing the bonds to my clutter. It saves space, time, and decision-making. How many dishes should you have? Two sets of everything are probably enough, though purists would insist that one is enough. Since I used to be a gourmet cook, I hung onto a whole drawer of rarely used utensils. If that's the worst clutter failure I have, I am doing pretty well.

Washing a ton of dishes can get depressing at first, so crank up that music! Imagine each dish as a victory. This is one area where taking a break can be counterproductive. Warm, soapy water is rather inviting. Cold, dirty, greasy dishwater is disgusting. Keep at it!

Now that the dishes are clean, let them air dry, unless you feel the need to get them put away immediately. I personally use the time to arrange the cabinets where they will live. As soon as they're dry, put them away! Leaving them in the drainer until you use them will invite another mess. The idea is that when you are finished, you have a clear countertop, clean dishes stored where you can find them, and a sense of pride.

Sinks and faucets

Nothing will give you more of a feeling of pride with less work than your clean sink with shining faucets in your decluttered kitchen. The faucets will gleam with very little work. Scrub them with cleansing powder, rinse them, and run a dry cloth over them to shine them. There, they look like new! Don't forget to scrub the gunk behind them. Once it is gone, it is easy to keep at bay.

Cabinets

While we are doing the kitchen, we might as well break the rule of "out of sight, leave it for later." You open these cabinets every day and seeing them organized will help your self-esteem. Don't get too organized, though. It will be good enough for now just to get rid of most of the junk in there. The flour that is a weevil colony should probably go first. Same with cornmeal. Coco-Puffs that no longer puff go in the garbage. Rice does seem to keep forever, though. (Personally, I used to hoard cookies. Part of my lack of consciousness was saving one or two cookies in a bag in case I could never get any again. When I ate one it tasted terrible, but I still put the sack back in the cupboard.)

Put the grains and pasta together. Canned goods can take forever to organize, so at first, just put all cans of a similar size in one place. You can work on this a little at a time. Cooking oils, flour etc. all go together. Or choose any system that makes sense to you, just don't over-complicate it. Now you have neat cabinets! Hopefully, they are a little less full than when you started.

Floors

You know what to do: Mop 'em. Sweep first though. (As a bachelor, I only recently learned that.) Rinsing is also a good idea. If you have pets, scrub their area. I swear my Fluffy appreciated it.

The Bathroom

You go there every day. Next to your bedroom, it is a place that sets the tone for your day. Fortunately, it is also the smallest and easiest to attack. Depending on how far gone it is, it should take only about 30 minutes to make a sizeable dent in it.

Toilet

"How can we rule a nation if we cannot clean our toilets."
—Mohandas Gandhi

Gandhi made this statement to a group of legislators in India before he left and literally cleaned toilets in the government palace. If he could do it, so can we.

Come on, let's start with the worst. It's the only throne most of us have. Soak the bowl in scouring powder while you scrub the tank. I use an old sock for the toilet and discard it afterwards. See, decluttering your socks was a good idea! When you are finished with the tank, scrub that handle! Shine it. It will make you feel good right away. The seat is probably not very nice-looking underneath. Shut your eyes if you have to, but clean it. The bowl will be ready to scrub. A toilet brush with a pointy end that cleans underneath the bowl is nice. Once the throne is done, stand back and give homage.

Sink, tub, and shower

The bathroom sink is easy. Scrub it and polish those handles. It will make you feel great every time you wash your hands or shave. The tub could probably use a bleach bath. The shower is probably moldy. Get some muriatic acid or an anti-mildew cleansers. Don't try to scrub it. When you are finished, shine those faucets.

Floors

Bathroom floors were designed to thwart mops. You are going to have to get on your hands and knees. You might as well pray while you are there.

Dining Room

Table

Most of us haven't seen the top of this table for years. All those important files are on top of it. Oh yeah, and the last three years of newspapers are there too. If you do crafts, there are probably several half-finished projects here. Done properly, this could be an easy job. Do it wrong and you will spend the rest of your life stuck on this item.

Start with the newspapers. Pitch them. Don't read them. You've got to be ruthless with newspapers. There will be a new one tomorrow. Start with a corner, rather than trying to wade into the middle of the heap. It's too depressing. Once you see some wood, you'll feel like a million bucks. If you find dirty dishes under a pile, don't stop to wash them. Put them into the sink and keep going. Dump those files into a banker's box or portable file cabinet and keep going. Dump those crafts projects into a box and keep going. Get the picture?

When you've got all the wood showing, polish it with furniture polish. Something about a shiny surface repels clutter.

China closets

Leave these alone until you have gotten the rest of the house together. They can take forever.

Floors

If you have a carpet, vacuum it. If you have tile floors, wash and wax them. If you have wood floors, mop them, wax them, and dance on them in celebration.

Living Room

Sofa

You probably have one, hidden under piles of books, magazines, and a few lost pets. This is really not a daunting task. Shelve the books (tips on that later). Ditch the newspapers and magazines. Free the dogs and cats.

Coffee tables and end tables

This should be easy by now. Clear them, clean them, polish them. Really, it is easier the more you get into it.

Bookcases

Tossing books is traumatic. I've left this for last, because next to filing, it is the hardest thing to do. Most people have a reverence for books, which I think is as it should be (speaking as a writer). Some books cannot be replaced. Some we read over and over again. Some are reference books and we rarely need them, but when we do, we do. So, I am there with you in spirit when you tackle this project. But remember, I did it and, while I did throw out some books I needed again, most of the stuff I do not miss. Accept that you are going to make mistakes. Just be honest. I had 14 Spanish dictionaries. There was no justification for that. I had guidebooks that were 10 years old. Russia has changed a bit since then. I tossed them.

You will probably not be able to discard more than a few at a time. Even with too many, you can make them neat. There might even have been some order to them to begin with. If not, take the time to create some. Just dump a bunch of them off a couple of shelves, so you will have a clean space to work with.

Establish broad categories, such as computers, self-help and spirituality, history, crafts, special interests (in my case Mexico and cigars), and so on. Fiction is a minefield. The danger is to sub-categorize these books into mysteries, serious fiction, Tom Clancy, etc. Don't do that. It doesn't matter what categories you make, just don't make too many. You can subcategorize later, and you will find it easier to discard useless books then.

Don't permanently attach labels to the shelves. Some categories will grow and others will shrink. Lightly tape papers with the categories to the shelves. You can always move them.

Ideally, if you have grown while doing these other exercises, you will be able to toss 25 percent of your books. If you are really good, you will get rid of half of them.

Stack the books vertically with the spine out. You'll get a lot more space and they will still look neat. The argument against this is that they are harder to get out. Come on, you probably don't get them out enough as it is. I keep mine like this even though I now have extra room. It's not really that hard to remove the book I want.

Finished!

We have gotten through your whole house. Doesn't it feel good! Chances are, we didn't do this overnight (but we could have, depending on your personal decluttering style). Most likely, it took days, weeks, or months. But we did it! Together. As we cleaned each area of your house, we cleaned your inner being. You are not only decluttered in your house, but in your soul as well. Now let's keep it up.

9 | The Spiritual View

The goal of decluttering is more than freeing ourselves from excess stuff in our lives. It is freeing ourselves from old ways of thinking that blocked the sunlight of the spirit from our souls. Our possessions were a physical manifestation of our limited, blocked lives. Our belief in lack, our fear-based mentality, and our lack of self-worth are all expressions of our distance from God. God wants us to be happy, prosperous, and free.

Purpose of Spirituality

The purpose of religion and spirituality is to achieve peace and harmony in this life. "How can one be at peace with a cluttered mind?" asks the Reverend Roger Aldi of the First Church of Religious Science in Houston, Texas. His spirituality is a wonderful amalgam of the practical, intellectual, and mystical. I met Roger in Burbank, California, before I started this book. Fate brought Roger and me both to Texas, within 50 miles of each other, so that he might share his wisdom with you and me. Coincidence? I believe that there are no coincidences in the Universe, only synchronicity.

Fear of Letting Go

"You must let go of a thing for a new one to come to you."

—Ralph Waldo Emerson

We clutterers are afraid to let go of our stuff because it involves risk, or a "lack of trust in life or God," as Rev. Aldi puts it. A person who believes that God will provide doesn't look to physical items to do the providing. He believes that his God or a Higher Power will take care of the details as long as he does the footwork.

There is an old story about a man whose house was being flooded by a river. An army humvee drove to him when the river was lapping at his porch and offered to get him out. He refused, saying, "The Lord will provide." The levee broke and he moved to the second floor. A Coast Guard rescue boat came by and offered to take him to higher ground. He refused, saying, "The Lord will provide." The water rose and rose and finally he was on the roof. An air force helicopter came by, dangling a ladder. He refused to climb up, saying, "The Lord will provide." Finally, he drowned. When he got to heaven, he asked God why He had forsaken him. "Come on, man, I sent the army, the Coast Guard and the air force! You gotta do your part."

We clutterers hold on to our possessions and our resentments, despite offers of help from many sources. We keep moving farther and farther away from help until only an act of God can save us, and we sometimes refuse that, too.

Not Just on the Physical Plane

"The universe can't bring anything new into our life
if we don't make some space."

—Rev. Roger Aldi

Cluttering is not just a matter of holding on to stuff on the physical plane. It is a reflection of our consciousness. We hold on to old grudges, old resentments, old loves, old disappointments. We make ourselves old and worn out before our time. If we carried all our junk on our backs day after day, we would soon have a bowed back, physical pain, and a sour disposition. What we manifest in the physical plane we first make real on the psychic plane. If we carry a spiritual suitcase of hurt and sadness, we will bow our soul's back, pinch our psychic nerves, and have a sour soul.

Few of us know how much old psychic stuff we are carrying around before we become enlightened. We think we can fix ourselves with more—more of everything physical—without realizing that having less inside will make us whole. We put our faith in a better job, more money, a better spouse, a bigger car, and so on. All the while, we are cluttering our souls with resentments because the job isn't really good enough, our neighbor has more money, our spouse doesn't fulfill all our needs, the car breaks down, and so on. We can manifest what we want and believe, but if our belief system is faulty, our manifestations will be too.

GOD—Good Orderly Direction

As I began to live more in recovery and less in squalor, I had to come face to face with my emotional baggage. I had to let go of it in order to make room for the good orderly life that I desired. I found out that I could not have a cluttered soul and a clean house. Sure, I could throw away lots of junk (and in fact, that is where most of us start), but I soon found that I still felt heavy. I tried to meditate, and did so in the best way I could at the time—which is to say a half-assed way.

I learned that one concentrates on breathing or a candle during meditation not because either of those has magical properties, but because they teach us how little we are able to concentrate on the here and now. I became aware of the mind-clutter that I was figuratively tripping over while trying to attain a higher consciousness.

Resentments

"In order to become cleansed and freed for many of life's problems, it is necessary to practice renunciation or release, especially in the human relations department."

—Catherine Ponder, *The Dynamic Laws of Prayer*

Self-help and 12-step programs believe that we heal by eliminating our resentments. When we begin to meditate and embark on a spiritual path, we find out how well we have done that. I found out that I hadn't done as good a job as I thought. But before you start to beat yourself up for that, (if indeed that is what you discover), remember that you did the best job you could at the time. The times have changed and so have you. As you proceed in your spiritual quest, you may have to backtrack in order to go forward.

Just as I try not to bring new clutter into my home, I try not to bring new clutter into my mind. I acknowledge resentments when they happen and let them lie around for a little while. Before they get too comfortable, I have to excise them. A psychologist pointed out that I may be 100 percent right 100 percent of the time, but life still doesn't always work out the way I want. Accept that and you have taken a huge step toward eliminating new resentments.

So what about the old resentments that have made nests in your cerebrum? They are comfortable. They have been with you for a long time. Therefore, you have to work on your resentments one at a time.

As a kid in South Texas, I worked with my father chopping Johnson grass from under the trees in our citrus grove. It was hot, sweaty work and I hated it. I hated my father for making me do it. I chopped the tall grass (often taller than I) at the base and went on. The old man said nothing. At the end of a week, he took me back to the trees I had first cleared. The weeds were already growing back. I'd thought they were gone forever. "Son," he said, "it don't do no good to hack away at just what you can see. You go to get to the roots, or you're just pissin' in the wind." Wise man, my father.

My resentment towards my father was one of my most rooted and strongest. Even after years of recovery from my alcoholism and attending meetings of Adult Children of Alcoholics, it was only when I began to recover from cluttering that I really, truly, faced him and unearthed the resentments I held for him. This came about while I was decluttering a box of my mother's memories. When I saw him as a man and not a demon, he ceased being able to demonize me. I let him go and I am sure that he, looking down from heaven, was glad to be set free. After that, my meditations were clearer.

Anne Sermons Gillis, author of *Offbeat Prayers for the Modern Mystic*, has a wonderful prayer. I've abbreviated it a little here, but it can be found in its entirety on page 84 of her book.

"Lord, I think that I am in prison because my mind keeps walking around the same little square....My longing to know more of the mental state is as deep as my commitment to self-realization. I wander closer and closer each day to my goal....Oh Lord of expectant beauty, lead me to freedom that I might break the beliefs that hold my mind in this tight restraint I call reality. Expand your infinite processes into my mind and guide me into the brilliance of everlasting light. Amen."

Surrender

Recovery programs suggest that we need to surrender to a Higher Power to get well. Whether you believe that your Higher Power is within you or outside of you, you must stop trying to fight the battle all alone. You have tried your way for years and have not conquered the problem. Maybe it is time to get back to God.

Christ taught that the kingdom of God was within us. Buddha taught that we can all recapture our original natures. The Tao states we can free our minds and return to the root. Zen philosophy teaches us that we are already complete. Our original natures are free from disorder. Only as we grow in our earthly confusion do we bring disorder and disharmony into our lives. By realigning ourselves with God, we realign ourselves with our true natures.

Letting Go to Win

*"In surrendering to one's own original sense of order and harmony,
one's compulsion is abated."*

—Mel Ash, *The Zen of Recovery*

In giving up our cluttering problem to a power greater than ourselves, we release ourselves from having to fight our compulsions alone. If we can leave our problems in God's hands, we can go about the business of working the solution. We must take practical steps to get rid of the outside mess and so we must take spiritual steps to get rid of the spiritual mess.

By letting go, we win greater freedom and happiness. By allying ourselves with a partner with infinite power, we magnify the effects of our own efforts. Through prayer and meditation, we gain strength to face each day and learn to concentrate on our successes and progress, rather than suffer in the guilt and denial.

As Franklin Roosevelt said, "We have nothing to fear but fear itself." Our fear kept us prisoners of our stuff and our stuffed mentality. Our new way of thinking and living will free us to return to our true natures, our God-like natures that have been hidden underneath our clutter.

Forgiveness

"Inner peace can be reached only when we practice forgiveness. Forgiveness is letting go of the past, and is therefore the means for correcting our misperceptions....Through true forgiveness we can stop the endless recycling of guilt and look upon ourselves and others with love. Forgiveness releases all thoughts that seem to separate ourselves from others. Without this belief in separation, we can accept our own healing and extend healing Love to all those around us."

—Gerald G. Jampolsky, from *Love is Letting Go of Fear*

Forgiveness is an important step in recovery. We learn to forgive ourselves for our imperfections and to forgive others for the hurts we feel they have caused us. We let go of the past to live in the present.

—❖—
Affirmations

© Clutterless (used by permission)

I live in a clutter-free environment, mentally, spiritually, emotionally.

I see beyond my clutter. I see the orderliness that lies within.

My life is filled with beauty and organization.

I am perfect as I am today. I constantly improve my definition of perfection.

I allow myself to be imperfect in the eyes of others, knowing I am perfect in the eyes of God.

Clutter is the past. Order is the present. Peace and prosperity are the future.

I start my day over whenever I need to.

God doesn't make junk. I do. With His help, I can get rid of it.

No task is overwhelming to me. I have the strength to overcome every challenge.

My finances are in perfect order.

There is always enough money in God's universe for my every need and want. I now claim my fair share.

Oops! I had a slip. It is not serious. If I can do it, I can undo it.

In God's perfect world, I am a perfect expression of God's love.

Time is a precious gift. I do not waste it on people, places, or things that do not deserve it.

Thank you, God, for the prosperity that right now flows to me as the rivers flow to the ocean and the ocean flows back to the shore.

The longest journey begins with the first step. I confidently take that step, knowing that I am guided in the right direction.

There is plenty in this world for me. I lovingly release those items that are no longer useful, knowing in truth that whatever I need shall be provided.

Money flows into my life according to the space I allow it.

As I love my pets, so God loves me. We both make mistakes, but they are temporary disruptions to the flow of God's love.

GOD—Good Orderly Direction, is my guide on this journey to orderliness.

Clean, clean, clean! That is my house!

Neat, neat, neat! That is my life!

—❖—

—❖—
Meditations
© Clutterless (used by permission)

1. *Thank you, God, for this perfect day ahead of me. I know that You will give me plenty of time to accomplish the tasks that are necessary, and the wisdom to know which they are.*

2. *I close my eyes and breathe the air or beauty and harmony that surrounds me. I go to that perfect place in my soul where the angels of neatness honor my presence. They love me and offer me their help in those times when I feel that I am alone. I am never alone. These angels are always beside me, guiding me, helping me. God's love is always with me. His angels are my constant companions.*

3. *Oh, Great Spirit, who created all things, teach me to honor and cherish your works. Teach me to respect what you have made by giving all my possessions the care and attention they deserve, not by hiding them or otherwise dishonoring them. All I have has been given to me by You, and I strive to show my gratitude by cherishing each item. If it gives me pleasure, I will give thanks. If it has outlived its usefulness to me, I will pass it on to others, who may yet receive joy from it. If it is worn out, broken, or useless, I ask Your help in discarding or recycling it, so that it may return in another form.*

4. *I visualize life as an enormous circle, without end or beginning. As I travel around it, I see that the road ahead is clean, orderly, and happy. If I look backward, and see the disorder I have left, I do not feel shame. That was but one point on my journey without end. I see the future as an unending series of points of clear lights, clear thoughts, clear spaces. Outside this circle that is my life, there are larger and larger circles,*

millions of them. They are the journeys of my fellows. Where we touch, we bring strength and harmony. My circle is one of many, not unique. If I have strength, I share it. If I am at a weak spot, another circle rushes to my aid. God's love is infinite. It is through others that He expresses His love. Today I will be an expression of perfect orderliness and calmness. Tomorrow, another may take my place. Circles within circles, lives within lives, we all touch and support each other. I am never alone.

10 | Financial Clutter

"Jesus did not have title to a foot of land and evidently had no money....He took it for granted that whatever He needed was His. He had the prosperity consciousness and proved that the earth with all its fullness does belong to the Lord, whose righteous sons are heirs to and in possession of all things."

—Emmett Fox, *Prosperity.*

Most clutterers have financial problems, regardless of their economic circumstances. They lose documents, bills, checks, and so on. They throw bills and other mail into a pile to get to "later." The bills go unpaid. The checks expire.

Although there are no hard statistics available from anonymous groups like CLA or DA (Debtor's Anonymous), my anecdotal research overwhelmingly indicated that clutterers have a serious problem with "debting" or "underearning," to use DA terms. "Underearning" means that many of us work at jobs that pay less than our skills could fetch, or, if we are self-employed, we charge less than our time is worth. These conditions stem from our feelings of not being as worthy as others or a "lack consciousness." Debtor's Anonymous has special meetings for debtors who are also clutterers. All of those attending these specialized meetings had faced up to the fact that their cluttering was affecting their financial life.

Of those attending clutterers' meetings, more than half alluded to debt problems. A third of them had tax problems stemming from ignoring property taxes, or non-filing or incomplete filing of income tax returns because their records were so disorganized that it was overwhelming to face. Because money is such a sensitive and private issue (even more so than cluttering), I suspect that the numbers are actually larger. Among the clutterers I interviewed (and myself) financial concerns were paramount. Only the more recovered were making any inroads into their financial morass. The information I present here is based on my unique perspective of having been a bill collector as well as someone behind on all of his bills, as well as on my conversations with other clutterers.

Crisis Forces Action

Webster's New World Dictionary and Thesaurus, 1997 online edition version 1.0, defines crisis as "the turning point of a disease for better or worse, esp. a sudden recovery; a turning point in the course of anything; decisive or crucial time, stage, or event."

Crisis is good! It forces us to direct our attention to the immediate source of discomfort. Because of our disorganization, pervasive sense of lack, and fear of letting go, we may have the money to pay our bills but be paralyzed and not do it.

My own finances vary wildly, as do those of many self-employed people. As the saying goes, "One day we eat chicken and the next day, feathers." One late night (why do we usually start doing these things after well-adjusted people are serenely tucked in bed?) during a "chicken" cycle, I rolled up my sleeves and waded into a pile of bills. When I called my creditors, I was surprised that I'd already taken care of most of them! I'd made a good situation into a fearful one by my disorganization.

Getting our finances under control takes time and hard work. It may be the most difficult task in recovery. Few of us like to face how we have spent our money. Many of us fear numbers. Details are boring. So now that we have gotten the excuses out of the way, let's do something about it.

Checking Accounts

I have had as many as four personal checking accounts at a time. When one got too mixed up, I switched. While that is not really facing the problem, it can be a good temporary fix. If your current account is too confusing to face, you can open a new one and start using it. Hooray for free checking! The important thing is to keep up with the new one. Make it easy on yourself and use carbon copy checks. If you do slip and forget to write a check in your register, you can fall back on the duplicate.

Many recovering clutterers have found that it easy to keep a new account uncluttered. Most of us don't write that many checks. We write our bills maybe twice a month. We make weekly or biweekly deposits. We can subtract. That's really all there is to it. So what was the big deal? We may not be ready for the answer yet.

What about that orphaned account? We can't just ignore it and let checks bounce. Put as much money as you can spare into it, as a cushion. Glance at it weekly. Don't try to figure it out yet, just make sure that no checks are bouncing. Add money if you need to. After six months, it should have settled down. Close it. Consider the extra money a gift from God. Treat yourself with it or use it to pay off a nagging bill. If the amount is large enough, do both.

Computer Programs

The advantage of using a computer program is that you can't write a check without entering it. You could just print a bunch of blank checks, but avoid the temptation. I have had to do that when traveling, and it usually results in trouble because I lose the slip of paper where I wrote down the amount and payee.

I've tried half a dozen computer financial programs. The most popular are: Intuit's Quicken, Microsoft Money, or Intuit's Quickbooks. They can help. One feature, a utility that reminds you when bills are due, is something to love or hate. It installs itself as a TSR (terminate and stay resident) program. That means it loads every time you start your computer. I disabled that feature on my computer (see Chapter 15 for detailed instructions), because it takes up base memory and degrades my computer's performance. These programs use preprinted checks, which will work for most people. If you have multiple businesses and one checking account, see the next section.

Computer Checks

I prefer a program that lets me print checks on blank stock. For years I used (and cursed) MIPS Inc.'s Versacheck and later Versacheck Web Pro Commerce. It is bulky and hard to get reports from, and technical support is worthless. But, I put up with it for the ability to use blank checks.

The MICR lines (those squiggly numbers at the bottom of your check) may not line up right. Take a check to your bank and see if they will process it. Alternative programs are My Checkwriter or My Business Checkwriter, both by My Software, Inc. These promise to work with Quicken, Microsoft Money, or Quickbooks. If they do, you are on easy street. If they don't, you are up the creek. There is no phone number for tech support.

Cash

Cash generates less clutter. Write a check to yourself for enough to last you for two weeks. Sure, you could use your ATM card, but are you going to remember to enter the amount in your register? Plus, you may pay for that privilege. If you insist on the ATM route, enter your withdrawal in your register before you leave the house. Debtors Anonymous recommends that people in its program get away from credit cards and use cash and checks exclusively. They also recommend that you keep a spending diary, so that you will know where your money goes. Bless your cash and your wallet. Keep the money neatly organized, instead of just stuffing it in.

Affirm Abundance With What You Have Right Now

Things may be better than you thought. What Jesus did with the loaves and fishes, we might be able to do with our loose change. Most of us have change lying around. I learned to put it into baggies, sorted by denomination (well, mostly). Once, when I was feeling poor, I took my treasure trove to the grocery store. I used the money to buy premium coffee beans, dog food, ice cream, and other comfort items. Sure, counting out $11 in nickels and dimes took some time, and the cashier was not all that thrilled, but it made me feel rich. I felt like I got these luxury items for free! Be kind to your fellow shoppers, and pick a non-busy time for your prosperity spree.

Most importantly, money started to flow back into my life from that point forward! The psychic law of supply and demand came into play. I blessed my supply and used it and more came to replace it.

Credit Cards

Oh joy! Oh woe! Credit cards are double-edged swords—great conveniences and great killers. Most of us have them, or at least can get secured ones. I myself have too many—way too many. Like many small businessmen, I used them to finance my businesses. Thank God I had them to use, or I might have had to get a real job (ugh!). Now I am paying for that privilege. And paying. And paying. If you are in this boat, get a bucket and start bailing.

A clutterer with lots of credit cards is a recipe for disaster. I didn't know how much plastic I had until I cleared up my finances.

Suze Orman and other financial writers suggest you should get rid of your credit cards. They say to keep only one for emergencies. DA suggests getting rid of them completely, though they will allow that an American Express card (which has to be paid in full every month) may be okay if you have learned some responsibility.

If you are not in serious credit card trouble, pat yourself on the back! Face your situation, get clarity, and take action. If you have a job and take responsibility for yourself, you can climb out of your hole before it becomes a grave. Learning to pay cash or to just not buy is a great freedom. Once you've gotten to the point where you throw something out for every new thing you bring in, you'll find it harder to bring things in. Once you get over the shame of having purchased a lot of junk, you will be less likely to get more.

But most of us are in trouble now and don't have the option of paying our cards off. So we slug away making the minimum payments, never getting ahead. I thought that credit cards would simplify my life and help me keep track of my expenses. And they can, for an organized person. I had dreams of scanning each month's statement into my computer (see Chapter 15 for more on that fallacy), or entering my purchases into Quickbooks. It didn't happen.

What did happen is that I spent without knowing what I owed. I never knew when bills were due and mislaid them when they came. Even though I had the money to pay them, they were late. This cost me a bundle in late charges. So here's a solution: As soon as you get a bill, write a check for it. If you don't have the money to pay it just then, put all the bills in the same place (I use a basket by the door). Write the date you have to mail it where the stamp goes. Check the bills every day and mail when necessary.

Dealing With Bill Collectors

Hard as it might be to believe, these men and women are people just like you and me. They have a job to do and you are the job. The problem is that their interest (separating you from your money) conflicts with your interest (holding on to it). Chances are, you know the bills are overdue. There is really no reason for them to call you, but they don't look at it that way. Having been a collector in a past life, I know that they are not all necessarily nice people. Some maladjusted personalities are attracted to this field because it gives them a feeling of power over others. I certainly was! And some of them, just like you and me, have bad days. So, be prepared for some of them to be nice to you and try to help you and for some of them to browbeat you. It's tough, but try to treat them as you would like to be treated. God will reward you, even if MegaBank Credit Card Services doesn't.

First of all, remember that without you, they wouldn't have a job. So, in a way, you are their employer! There, doesn't that make you feel better? Remember that they would rather deal with a nice person than a nasty person. If you are nice, you are likely to elicit a nice response. Don't hide. Call them. The ones with the credit card companies are usually nice to deal with. They like dates and amounts, but don't just agree to whatever they want. Tell them what you can do.

Try not to agree to what they ask if you can't follow through. They hate broken promises. Offer them something. But use common sense. Some people say that if you pay them "something" they will appreciate it. That might have been true in the old days, but not with bank cards today. Hospitals, doctors, anyone you owe personally, and small companies will appreciate partial payments. Credit card companies have a formula for calculating delinquency. If you don't pay the minimum amount, you will be, as one collector stated to me, "just giving us money." If you have $10 available, send it to someone you only owe a little, not someone you owe $100.

Options for Getting Out of Debt

1. Equity loans

If you are a homeowner, you can borrow against your equity. That may be the best choice, but if you do not get your financial cluttering under control, you will be back where you started, and homeless to boot! But, it you are honest about cleaning up your act, this relives all the stress and gives you room to breathe without affecting your credit. Think carefully and be honest. If your intentions are to pay off your debts and not incur more, this could be your best bet. The pitfall here is that unless you use this breather to declutter your finances, you can end up worse off than when you started. If you don't clean your financial house, you can lose your physical house. What often happens is that before long, those who get these loans are overextended with credit card debt, plus they now have a second mortgage. This produces a double whammy, both emotionally and spiritually. Believe me, I was involved in this part of the financial world when it first started. I've seen too many people who ended up in worse trouble than they were in when they started.

2. Hardship programs

Few collectors will tell you this, but most credit card companies have plans that enable you to pay a smaller amount and reduce the amount of interest on your debt. These plans may be called "hardship," "curing," or "extension" programs. Banks have them too.

I got a shock when I called one company late at night, responding to a collector who had called me earlier in the day. She told me that if I would pay the past due, she could extend the next payment for five days. I asked the night guy about this and told him my cash-flow situation. He said that I qualified for a "self-cure" program whereby I paid

$50 a month instead of the $150 that was due. At the end of three months the account would be current! If I had hidden from the collectors (the natural tendency for clutterers), I would never have found out about this plan.

The deal is that you have to convince the credit card company that you are only temporarily in trouble and not just a deadbeat. Sometimes they want last year's tax statement, which few clutterers have, or can find. Some companies will waive that if you explain your situation.

If you qualify for one of these programs, you can stop the collection calls and letters and keep the account (though it will be closed). You'll pay about one-third to one-half of what you used to pay. The disadvantage is that your credit report reflects "account closed by creditor." But that doesn't stay on there forever. If you keep up the payments, the account may be reopened. Most important, you'll feel better about yourself for trying. If you default on the agreement for more than a couple of months, they will kick you out of the program and you will be back to square one. However, it beats bankruptcy.

3. Consumer credit counseling services

Another alternative is Consumer Credit Counseling Services. They are a nonprofit organization and will negotiate a low payment for you. Your credit report will show that you went into a CCCS program. Also, if you miss a payment, they can kick you out of the program and you are back to being way behind. Additionally, your account will be at a collection agency. They require you to cut up all your credit cards. Maybe that is not a bad idea, but I prefer trying the alternative above. It at least gives you some responsibility and control.

4. Bankruptcy

Bankruptcy may be the best option, but it usually isn't. I considered it and a nice lawyer told me there was a 90 day waiting period. "A lot can happen in 90 days," she said. She was right.

That was a year ago. Things got better. I caught up. I got ahead. Then I got behind again. My travel agency is seasonal and the summer is the worst season. Come winter, I was ahead.

Bankruptcy is the last alternative. It does mar your credit, but it certainly relieves a lot of stress. Think carefully about it. Talk to a lawyer for the details, and try to find one who doesn't want to push you into it. Ask yourself in a quiet moment if your financial problems are due to your hoarding and cluttering. If you can work on that, and increase your prosperity consciousness, you can work your way out.

Scams

One scam I nearly fell for was to sign up with a company that offered to negotiate with my creditors. They wanted to charge me a percentage of my outstanding debt! Their "services" were nothing more than I could negotiate for myself—without a fee! So give them a wide berth.

Now my e-mail inbox is flooded with offers like this. Apparently more companies are realizing that there is a sucker born every minute. These scam artists are now advertising on TV. They are vultures and should be shunned. CCCS or even bankruptcy is preferable to giving your money to these bloodsuckers.

There are some legitimate non-profit credit consolidation companyes. But there are some scams, too. Buyer beware.

Conclusion

No matter what our financial situations, when we face them, we can deal with them. No matter how prosperous or limited we may be, it is only temporary. I have been a millionaire twice in my life and I have lived on nothing but rice and peppers a few times. What I've learned from this is that money comes and goes, but who I am is not what I have.

11 | Prosperity Is an Inside Job

"I am come that they might have life and have it more abundantly."
—John 10:10

Clutterers often have a "lack" mentality. We believe that we will never have enough, that what we have will not be replaced if taken away, and that we do not deserve better—more, perhaps, but not better. But we can change this thinking as we recover.

A universal truth is that we get what we believe we deserve. If we believe that we don't deserve the best, that we don't deserve a full and rich personal life with adequate material possessions, we will hoard those pitiful ones that we do have.

Be Grateful For What You Have Right Now!

Get grateful. We begin by realizing how prosperous we already are. Prosperity is not just stuff. It is people, health, pets, how we feel. When we have decluttered our house and found all that loose change, we celebrate that. If you are like me and find $700, accept that this is a gift from God that you ignored. Do you have a roof over your head? Enough food? Someone who loves you? A pet that loves you? (If you have a dog or a bird, definitely. If you have a cat, well, maybe.)

Spiritual teachers like Jesus, Tao, Buddha, Ernest Holmes, Catherine Ponder, Emmett Fox, Eric Butterworth, Ralph Waldo Emerson, and on and on have told us that God will provide, and provide abundantly. Practical teachers like Norman Vincent Peale, Og Mandingo, Dale Carnegie, Tony Robbins, Suze Orman and countless others have told us, and demonstrated in their own lives, that if we change our minds, we can change our lives.

The Difference Between a Rut and a Grave

Okay, you're sitting in a messy house, surrounded by things that are treasures to you and trash to others. You're probably depressed. Your finances are a mess. You are alone. So how do you get out of your rut?

Sometimes it's hard to get grateful when surrounded by chaos. Getting out of our cluttered surroundings is always good. I like to go to a museum, where beauty and order can lift my spirits. Parks bring me closer to nature and the things that matter. Another tool is to read books that will point you in the right direction. Any of Catherine Ponder's books are a good start. I especially like *The Dynamic Laws of Prosperity* as a beginning. She is easy to read and very practical. You don't have to believe, just have an open mind. Tony Robbins is dynamic and powerful and his books and tapes have helped millions. Suze Orman is very practical and can help you get your financial affairs in order. Her books are uplifting and filled with no-nonsense prosperity tips.

Associate With Positive People

Check out social organizations like Optimists, Lions, Kiwanis, and so on, or a self-help group like Clutterless *(www.clutter-recovery.com)*. Prosperity consciousness is a large part of their core belief and approach to recovery from cluttering.

It is best to be selective in telling your current friends that you are changing your life. Chances are you are associating with negative people. Such people love to bring others down to their level. So whenever people start talking about how hard times are, or how little they have, change the subject or walk away. It does no good, at this stage of your development, to try to enlighten others. Their negativity will overwhelm you.

The Spiritual or Religious Approach

You may not believe in God, or you may have soured on the religion of your youth. I was the same way. But when at the end of my tether, I decided to give God another chance, it paid off in many ways.

If you are led to try a spiritual or religious approach, great. If your search leads you to a group or church that believes in positive thinking, so much the better. I personally like Religious Science, Science of Mind, and Unity, the three most established New Thought religions, with membership in the hundreds of thousands, worldwide. Each uses a somewhat different approach, but they all believe that man is meant to be happy and to live in a positive manner. They do not agree with the guilt concept common in some mainstream religions. They all believe that man makes choices in life to be happy and fulfilled or not. They believe in the teachings of Jesus, as well as those of Buddha, Tao, Emmet Fox, Emerson, and other philosophers. If you are happy with your established church or synagogue and get spiritual nourishment from it, great. The important thing is to find one that speaks to you. It is probably best to avoid those that teach lack and sin. Start believing that it is good to have material goods, just not as many as you have right now.

Change may not occur overnight, but it can. Science of Mind groups (which is *not* related to Christian Science or Scientology) start their services with, "Welcome to Science of Mind, where we only ask that you change your mind and change your life." Most likely, you will have to start manifesting your new life a little at a time. Read the affirmations in Chapter 9. Read them as often as you want. If you really want to change, they will sink in. In *Unlimited Power*, Tony Robbins writes, "The world we live in is the world we choose to live in. If we choose bliss, that's what we get. If we choose misery, we get that too."

Money Flows

Money flows like a big river into an ocean of abundance. It cannot flow into a cluttered home or mind. You have got to take the physical action first to get the flow going. Imagine, as you declutter, that the pathways you open up in your home are riverbeds of prosperity. From a very practical standpoint, you can prove that to yourself if you have a garage sale with the things you eliminate from your life. If the garage sale is just too difficult for you, it is better to just get rid of things. When you donate them to the Salvation Army or Goodwill, get a receipt for their true value. Treasure this like a check. It is a check—from the IRS. See, already, prosperity has flowed into your life!

Part of prosperity is giving. Norman Vincent Peale said that giving is the secret of the law of abundance. "To receive the good things of life, you must first give." It is part of the natural flow of money. It flows into your life and you let it flow out. More flows back, 10 times more than you give. Jesus proved this with the loaves and the fishes and countless other teachings. If your funds are low, give of your time.

When I first started going to church, I could squeeze out a dollar for the collection plate. It hurt. As I grew in prosperity consciousness, I realized that giving has to be done with a glad heart. A wonderful Religious Science minister, Rev. Marlene Morris, in Burbank, California, made it clear to me. She said not to tithe a certain amount until you were comfortable with it. If you give a large amount (to a church, organization, or individual) because you feel you have to, you will not reap any reward from it. She said she would rather someone gave a dollar with a glad heart than a $100 grudgingly. Wow! A preacher who didn't make me feel guilty unless I helped buy a new rectory! But, she said, you get back what you give. You get back 10 times what you give, so if you want only $10 back, then give a dollar. Heck, I could do the math. I gladly dropped $2 into the plate. And guess what? I got an unexpected $20 in the mail shortly thereafter!

It doesn't always work like that, but it has worked like that often enough for me to keep it up. I know that whatever I get, I must give back to keep the flow going.

Money is not the only thing you can give to get the flow going. Give of your time. But be careful to give what you can give with an easy heart. Clutterers often over-commit and don't make enough time for themselves. So make your first gift of time to yourself—for enjoyment. Go to the beach. Go to the park. Go to Tahiti. Just go. Then you can give to someone who needs the services you can offer.

Pray

Pray for prosperity. Make God your business partner. Every morning, I meditate and pray to God for money to flow in. Sometimes, the flow is restricted, but I try my best not to get nervous about it. I believe that it will flow and it always has. Sure, there are people who insist that you are not to pray for yourself, or for material things. Let them think as they want. Even Jesus prayed for specific results. Bless your wallet or purse or checkbook. Hold it in your hand and say, "God, I bless this abundance represented here and am grateful for the continuing abundance that flows into it, 10 times over." It will take a while, but you will believe it once it starts happening.

A Prosperity Wheel

Got a dream? Make a prosperity wheel by drawing a circle on a large sheet of poster paper. Divide the circle into quarters. Label them personal, financial, spiritual, and physical. Then cut out pictures (from the magazines you have been hoarding) of something that represents each area of your life. Tape them to the wheel. Look at it every day, as often as you want. Say, "Thank you God, for [item], or something better, that is here, right now, in my life, and serves my higher good."

This will feel funny at first. How can you say something *is* when it clearly *is not*? The Universe can only say yes. It only knows the now. When you say something is, you tell the Universe to create it. Never vacillate with the Universe. Things are. If a loving relationship is what you desire, put up a picture of what a loving relationship looks like to you. Picture the way it should be in your mind. Picture the person. Feel the emotions of love that radiate between you and that person find each other.

If it is money that you desire, be specific. Don't say, "a lot of money." The Universe doesn't know what that means. To some people, $100 is a lot of money. To others it is $100,000. You can start with any amount that feels comfortable for you. Just make sure that it is an amount that you truly believe you deserve and can handle. A million dollars tomorrow might be too much for your consciousness. You might only be able to be responsible for $1,000 or a $100. You can always up the ante.

Gambling

We are all gamblers in something. My experiences with gambling are only for examples of prosperity thinking in action, but you can substitute investments, putting the money into your own business, or whatever form of financial risk you feel comfortable with. The principles are universal. Money is not the object. Acceptance of money is the object.

I am a gambler. Not a big time gambler; not a compulsive gambler, just a gambler. I speculate in the options market. I shoot craps. I generally win. I won even before I encountered prosperity thinking. After encountering this belief system, I went to Vegas affirming that I would come back with $10,000. I took $100 with me. I bought $20 in chips. At one point, I was ahead about $600. My gut told me to quit. But I thought it would be disloyal to the Universe not to get *my* 10-fold increase. The table turned cold. I realized that, no matter how I affirmed, the flow of money was going *from* me *to* the casino. I left. I had $220 after expenses. That was 10 times what I really felt comfortable risking. I gave $20 to charity.

I wasn't ready to win $10,000. Even though I had affirmed that amount, it was not real to my subconscious. Now I affirm $1,000 and generally win $600. But I am only comfortable risking $200 at a time. For me, in this area of my life, I have gotten stuck on three times my risk. It ain't the Universe's fault. It is my consciousness. The important thing is, I believe I will be a winner and I am. Don't be rigid. Take what the Universe freely gives you, and when that particular experience in your life turns cold, collect your winnings and walk away a winner.

I don't always win money, but I always win. This isn't a get-rich-quick scheme, so don't clean out the bank account and rush to Vegas (or Louisiana or wherever is close). The Universe taught me a very valuable lesson the last time I went to Vegas. I dressed like a winner in my cashmere car coat, slacks, polo shirt, and leather shoes. I got a Jacuzzi suite. I thought like a winner. I allocated $600 to risk. I lost $480 and called it quits. The lesson that I was to learn was to have fun.

Rx: Have Fun

Most clutterers are afraid to have fun. Having fun means letting go and that goes against our grain. I had far more fun losing that $480 than I ever had winning money. When I lost that money, I learned to enjoy playing the game. The game became the reason for playing and money became the byproduct. Before, when I was so uptight about losing what I had gained, I was operating from fear and *felt* like a loser. When I learned to enjoy myself, I *felt* like a winner. Money is not what makes me happy. Ever since that incident and the accompanying shift in my consciousness, I have always won money in casinos. Now, winning money is my expected outcome. More importantly, I have a great deal of fun doing it.

Money is not what makes me happy. Money is a byproduct of being happy. Remember that. Money is not God. God is God. When we know that, and accept that, God can co-create whatever is for our highest and best good. Now, when I gamble, I have a ball. I yell and scream and joke with the pit bosses and stickmen and players and really enjoy myself. I have recouped my losses and am ahead financially, but more importantly, I am ahead in happiness. Learning to have fun was well worth the financial payment I made. When I play the options market, I shout, "Go, baby, go," when my stock is going the right way. I enjoy the drama and excitement and being a part of it.

What Is Success?

Norman Vincent Peale, in *The Amazing Results of Positive Thinking*, defined success as "not mere achievement, but rather the more difficult feat of handling your life efficiently. It means to be a success as a person; controlled, organized, not part of the world's problems, but part of its cure....of being creative individuals."

Affirm for yourself that you *are* a success. Affirm that you are successful in getting rid of your clutter. If you are having a hard time getting started, be grateful that you are such a successful clutterer. Who else could have amassed such a collection of stuff?!

12 | Sex, Relationships, and Family

I used to joke that I didn't know much about sex because I was married. Married or not, many clutterers confided in me that their sex lives were unsatisfying. Although a study in the *Journal of Sex and Marital Therapy* indicated that 80 percent of OCD marriages were "significantly troubled," there are other studies that show that OCD marriages are about as happy as any other.

One psychiatrist whom I spoke with summed up the complexity of this issue. "In most cases, no one bothers to get baseline data about sexual activity. An incapacitating case of hoarding or cluttering would make a successful sex life difficult—the individual is preoccupied with the pathologic behavior, and potential partners would be put off. It is not safe to say that people in treatment have little sex life—it depends on how they cope with sexual side-effects and whether the particular individual experiences them."

Relationships

Married clutterers have a real dilemma. Most of them had not progressed far in their disease when they married and formed strong relationships with their spouses. Later, as the disease took over, the spouse (like the spouses of alcoholics), just kept hoping it would get better. As the husband of a clutterer said to me, "You don't throw someone away like a broken toy when they become sick. You still love them. You do the best you can, even when you don't know what to do. Finally, you just give up and hope for a miracle." (One man diagnosed with OCD told me that he didn't see how someone could live with a hoarder and not become one. His example was that his wife (who was the hoarder) started to collect hub cabs. Gradually he began stopping on the freeway to pick up hubcaps to bring to her.)

Nagging often becomes the tool of choice for the non-clutterer. "If you would just listen to me, things would be better. Why can't you just take my advice?" Anyone who has ever lived with a nagging spouse knows how much sexual attraction there is in such a relationship. The clutterer hears the "gentle suggestions" as disapproval and feels misunderstood. The clutterer also often feels that he or she can punish the nagging spouse by continuing the behavior.

Separate Bedrooms

Separate bedrooms often seem to be a solution. That was certainly advocated by my last ex-wife, who was obsessively neat and tidy. She couldn't work because she needed the time to make everything just so. I enabled her, not because I enjoyed living in a neat house (it really made no difference to me), but because my self-esteem was so shot that I would have done anything (short of decluttering) to keep such a beautiful woman from leaving me. So I worked a full-time job and wrote computer programs at night. That left little time for enjoying each other.

As the relationship matured (or rotted), the nagging increased. My computer room was the only place in the house where I felt I had any control. Even so, she periodically made "neat sweeps" and neatened it up. I felt betrayed and violated afterwards. "I did it for your own good," she would assert. I usually said nothing and retreated into my world of bits and bytes. Our sex life, which started out hotter than the 4th of July, became the winter of our discontent. This experience is pretty typical among clutterers married to normal people.

Clutterers Married to Each Other

For clutterers married to each other, there is a similar dance. Each one sees the other's clutter as loathsome and will be sure to point that out. The complaining, self-righteous one will soon blame his or her clutter on the weaker one: "If only you weren't such a slob, I could clean up this mess." "Your clutter is as bad as mine." "No it isn't." "Yes it is." Nah, nah, nah. And so it goes. Separate bedrooms are a requirement in such households because there is only space for one person in any bed. If the couple lives in a one-bedroom apartment, one spouse ends up on the couch permanently. The couch becomes a nest, adding impossibility to the common area. If one spouse starts to clean up, the other will mess it up out of spite, like crabs in a bucket that pull any crab trying to make a break for it back into the bucket.

Recovering Couples

I have seen some couples recover. If only one is a hoarder, then joining the self-help Clutterless or the 12-step Clutterers Anonymous group can work. If both are clutterers/hoarders, they both have to get into the program. Because the dynamics here are so intertwined, like vines that have grown so twisted together that you cannot tell where one begins and another ends, couples' therapy is often required.

Couples may want to join RCA, Recovering Couples Anonymous (*www.recovering-couples.org*). It is a 12-step program for couples who are in another 12-step program and have realized that their relationship is as sick as they once were. Many of the couples in RCA have tried therapy without success. They come to RCA in a last-ditch effort to save their relationship. It is a difficult program. You have to face both yourself and your relationship as they are, as you have created them. You have to take mutual responsibility for what your relationship has become.

In RCA, you learn that you have brought the dysfunctions of your addictions into the relationship. Then you have to do something about it. You will meet hoarders, alcoholics, drug addicts, sex addicts, people with OCD, overeaters, and so on there. The surprising thing is that RCA works for many people, both gay and straight. It is a program for those who have already made some progress with their individual addictions. If you are willing to work at making a twisted relationship into a flowering, loving relationship again, it might work for you. It has worked for others.

Dating

Remember when I mentioned that our beds are usually littered with books, magazines, dirty dishes, clothes, and so on? It doesn't take a Ph.D. in psychology to figure out that this is a great way to avoid intimacy. Can you imagine meeting the man or woman of your dreams at a party, dazzling him or her with your wit and charm, and then inviting him or her to a boudoir that is more like a garbage dump? To even get there they would have to traverse the minefield of your living room, being careful to stay on the poorly-marked paths to the bedroom. Forget it! Mood is everything in seduction, and you can't light candles because you might burn the place down.

That said, I have to admit that I did lure unsuspecting women to my hovel. Most never returned. Some wonderful and enabling souls tried to make real relationships with me, and even helped me clean up. It was fruitless. Within a week the bedroom would be a nest again. (One clutterer, whose problem had not become completely overwhelming, told me, "Hell, if it wasn't for dates, my house would never get picked up.") My most enduring relationships were with women who traveled with me when I was on the road for weeks at a time, were married, or lived in another state.

I thought that one-night stands were just my fate. I created that reality. Now that I have a little psychological awareness, I realize that I was using my clutter as a way to make sure that no real intimacy ever developed.

Most clutterers I have talked to have such low self-esteem that they don't really date. They are so ashamed of the way they live that they do not invite even friends over, much less dates. Yet, most clutterers are really nice people, very caring and supportive. They would make wonderful mates. They are sensitive and, though they have isolated themselves, would secretly love to have a relationship with something other than their clutter. Our problem is that we have replaced people with things. We have denied ourselves love by surrounding ourselves with our self-loathing. We have traded intimacy for monuments to our insecurity.

Sex Life a Benefit of Recovery!

One more motivation for hoarders to keep up their recovery efforts is that one of the benefits at the end of the tunnel is an improved sex life. Sex is a powerful motivator. That, combined with the money motivation that comes with abundance thinking should be powerful enough to help many clutterers stay on track. With sex often comes love. From that springs a relationship. Gosh, if we could just control our compulsion to hoard, we could have the same kind of normal family lives that the rest of the world has. If we could keep that in mind, we might find recovery to be a lot easier.

Some people taking SSRIs may experience a decrease in the libido. If you have a therapist, discuss it frankly. If you have a spouse or partner, involve him or her in the discussion. Remember, drug therapy is not necessarily permanent. And some of us are oversexed anyway, so it doesn't always mean that our sex lives go to pot.

Sex Is Spiritual

If you and your therapist have decided that you need medication, use the time to work on learning how to be intimate with another person on an emotional and spiritual level. Having been there and done that, I can attest that sexual fulfillment becomes far more fulfilling as a result of that work. In fact, that is a worthy goal of every person, OCD or not, taking medication or not.

Sex is a natural, wonderful act and can be a spiritual experience as well. Taoist teachers talk about the Tao of sex. I myself cannot envision a life without sex. But many of us clutterers have built such prisons around ourselves that we have sentenced ourselves to a life of celibacy. Whatever it takes to break out of those cold stone walls is worth doing, in my opinion. Some people have voluntarily chosen a life of celibacy. If that is your choice, and it brings you happiness and fulfillment, then don't feel guilty that the sexual path is not for you. My only point here is that we can learn to make these decisions for ourselves and not give up our power to our hoarding.

13 | What Recovery Feels Like

While writing this book, I reached a new level of my own recovery. In my interviews with other clutterers, I learned what it felt like to them. These might be called the "promises" of taking the action and seeing the results.

The Promises

© *Clutterless (used by permission)*

1. You will know more happiness and freedom from worry.
2. You will know the joy of not having to hide your shame.
3. You will feel more self-confident and secure.
4. You will feel like a whole new world has opened up to you.
5. You will stop beating yourself up for your disease.
6. You will stop blaming others for what is your responsibility.

7. You will stop being afraid of having people know the real you.
8. You will develop a more spiritual manner of living, which will help you in all areas of your life.
9. You will want to share your experiences with others, to help them and you.
10. You will accept your imperfections as expressions of your humanity.

Pie in the sky? I don't think so. My experience and that of my fellow clutterers has proven these promises again and again.

The strangest thing may turn the corner for you. When I bought my espresso machine, it was an expression of abundance and validation that I was worth the best. When I lived in Seattle, I would press my nose against the glass and envy all those rich people in Starbucks. Years later, buying a silly little thing like an espresso machine got me out of my poverty thinking and invalidated *that* old tape. Once I had it, I had to clean it every night to enjoy the freshly-ground taste that I have come to appreciate. While doing that at night, I figure I might as well wash the rest of the dishes. The end result is that I get up feeling rich, and recovered, when I go into my clean kitchen. No matter what else I let slide, the dishes are always washed. Like clutter, this neatness spills over into other parts of my life.

I've found that when I have a clear space anywhere in the house that I see every day, I abhor defiling it with clutter. Perhaps this is where the compulsive part of my personality shows up. I can no longer begin work with my cluttered desk. I have to clear it off, wipe it down and straighten it up every night before I retire. At first, this was exceedingly hard. I liken it to the time when I was a weight-trainer. I liken that experience to recovery from flabbiness.

The first few times of lifting weights brought me an exhilaration that made me want to keep it up. After a few months, I saw the results of my work in increased biceps, the feeling of power and well-being that coursed through my body. This success made me slack off. After all, what would it matter if I skipped a session? I could always make it up the next day.

I couldn't. It was harder and harder to face the regimen of lifting those plates of iron after a few days. What had been joy was now distasteful. What had been effortless became painful. Eventually, I stopped training. My muscles withered. In a few weeks, all my work had been undone. I was once again a flabby middle-aged man. I felt even worse about seeing myself in the mirror because I had had a taste of what I could be like.

No Excuses

So it is with recovery from cluttering. I work late, often until 3 a.m. I quit when I am too tired to write anymore. Bed beckons. The desk is a mess, with books, notes, tapes, and cigar ashes. At first, I cleaned up the wreckage religiously. Then I slacked off. After all, what would it matter if I left it until tomorrow? I could clean it up in the morning. Morning came, and, as I have other businesses to run, calls come in, things need to be dealt with, and there doesn't seem to be enough time to clear off the desk. I say I will do it at the end of the work day. At the end of the day, I am tired. All I want to do is get out of the office and walk my dog on the beach. (Most of you will replace that phrase with "get into my car and go home.") So the desk waits, patiently collecting clutter until I arrive the next day. And so on. Once the wrong road is taken, it takes more work to get back than it took to get there in the first place.

Dishes are a perfect example. How many people do you know who say they love to do the dishes? Even your neat friends will tell you they hate to do the dishes. That is why they got a dishwasher. Forget about the ones who say they got a maid. They are weird.

I have had dishwashers and I've lived without them. It didn't seem to make much difference. The dishes piled up until I could scrape them when I had a dishwasher, and they piled up until I could wash them when I didn't. When I absolutely had to have a clean plate, I would resentfully scrape one off, run an enormous amount of hot water over it to kill the new strains of germs that had been growing on it, and leave the rest until later.

A Clean Kitchen Serves Up Big Rewards

There is probably no other area of your home where changing your habits will have a more freeing effect on you than your kitchen. And it is one of the easiest areas to change! Really! There is no one thing that will bring you more joy and help you start your day in a much better mood, than walking into a clean kitchen. If you are a coffee drinker, imagine the ease of just turning on your pot with the coffee all ready to go! What was once a chore will become a pleasure.

One weekend, I got into a cleaning frenzy and went beyond decluttering. I scrubbed the floors on my hands and knees (which wouldn't have been necessary if had been willing to spend $15 for a mop). However, I rationalized that I would see how often I used it before I invested that much money in something that would provide so little pleasure. I'd have no qualms about spending that and more for a book, computer program, or just about anything else (except a visit to the dentist).

So I scrubbed the kitchen sinks, the floor, the stove, and the refrigerator (the outside anyway – one shouldn't get too carried away), washed all the dishes (including the ones lurking in other rooms), scrubbed the tub, bathroom sink, floor, and cabinets, vacuumed the carpet, straightened up the bookcase, threw away clothes that were past their prime, and neatened up in general. Whew! I was exhausted and proud when that day was over.

I should add that you can't do these things until you have already made a healthy attack on your clutter. If you start too soon with a program like this, you might vacuum up the cat or a small child you can't see in all the piles.

Start Your Day With Joy, Not Pain

My morning routine is to drink some coffee, smoke a fresh cigar, and meditate in the bathtub. The quality of my meditation improved dramatically once my mind was clear of resentments and guilt over my clutter.

At night, I grind my coffee for the next day and put it into my two coffee makers (typical clutterer, I have an espresso machine and a regular coffee maker). When I wake in the morning, still sleepy-headed, I stumble directly for the coffee. Wow! I just turn it on and trundle off to draw my bath. What used to be a chore is a pleasure. The immediate gratification is two-fold. First of all, I feel peace instead of guilt when I walk into a clean kitchen. Second, instead of starting my day off with a chore, I start it off with ease. Instead of grumbling about having to get the beans out of the fridge, pour them into the grinder (generally spilling one-third of them because my motor skills haven't yet revved up), dumping the old grounds, washing the pot, and finally starting the process that will bring me back to the living, I am rewarded with the smell of freshly-ground coffee brewing within a minute.

Doing It Now Saves Time

I do the dishes every day. Perhaps I have become obsessive about it, but it is much better than the way it used to be. After a meal, I wash the dirty dishes. I used to put this off, believing it took too much time, so I had to prove to myself that this was not true. I timed how long it takes to clean up after lunch for two people—three to six minutes. Dinner for two, 12 to 15 minutes. When I let it go until I absolutely had to wash again (a couple of lunches and a dinner), it took 38 to 46 minutes. Done right away, three meals took 18 to 27 minutes. Doing it later took longer because first I had to scrape the dishes, get them out of the sink, scrub the sink for lurking bacteria from the dishes, and dig in. Lunch for one—a plate, knife, fork, and glass—takes less than one minute. Come on, why waste your precious time? Take care of things right away and you'll have more time for more important or enjoyable things. A recovering clutterer has a sign over her sink that reads, "I am planting minutes now to harvest hours on my weekend."

You cannot quantify the general feeling of distaste you feel when you walk into a dirty kitchen, or the guilt you feel for slipping into old habits. To help keep yourself from slipping, cut down on the number of dishes you have. I now have seven plates (three for daily use and four china), four place settings of silverware, eight pots and pans of varying sizes, five bowls, and way too many glasses and cups. I justify this by the fact that I now have company come over and barbecues in the backyard.

Let's say you don't do the dishes every time you use them. Another way to get them done and feel like you are saving time is to start them when you have another project going that doesn't require your full attention. When you turn on your computer, it takes awhile to load. I've found that doing the dishes, or some other decluttering chore, can often be accomplished by the time the computer is ready to roll. There, you've killed two birds with one stone!

Books and Videos

If you've reached this chapter, you probably have gone through all your books and videos and discarded about 30 percent of them. Guess what? If you go through them again, you'll find another 10 to 20 percent that you really don't need after all. Moreover, your new acquisitions will have aged properly so that you can consider discarding some of them.

One thing you can do on the second pass is to really organize your books. I thought I'd done a good job, but today, when I had to rearrange the front room and move a bookcase, I found that many of the books I had needed since moving had been there all the time, just misfiled. This second hit gave me the chance to put like with like. All my B. Traven novels were reunited, and my Russian language course joined its fellows in Spanish and French. True, others will say that you should discard them, as the odds are against your learning those languages now, but sometimes you have to cut yourself some slack. Hope springs eternal.

We all have our hardheaded spots. That is why someone can help you get started, but the really hard part is yours to do alone. I truly believe that I will make the time to learn these languages someday (oops, I seem to have used that dreaded clutterer excuse—"someday"). Let me live with the fantasy. I have made such progress that I am allowed a few indiscretions. In fact, I met a Russian person and wanted to learn a few words to break the ice the next time we met. If I'd been able to find my Russian language book, I could have.

Your Car

I knew a clutterer who sold his car rather than clean it! I've known others who could barely squeeze in to drive. Not only is this uncomfortable, it is dangerous. Make a sudden stop and things will fly all over the place.

The car is the easiest to clean and the last thing we'll cover. A trip to a car wash (I recommend doing it yourself for the feeling of accomplishment you'll get) and a vacuum will do wonders. I put all the stuff I think I need (extra water, coolant, jumper cables, and so on) in a plastic bin with a flip top and put it in the back. That's pretty much it. But it will make you feel wonderful and recovered when you drive anywhere. Imagine being able to actually give someone a ride!

The Lighter Promises

1. *You will no longer fear repairmen—just their bills.*

2. *You will be able to go to the bathroom at night without fear of falling over something.*

3. *You will actually be able to shut the door to your bedroom, if not the past.*

4. *You will not have to invent excuses for your mess; freeing yourself to find new things to invent excuses for.*

5. *You will know where your keys are, especially useful after you have locked yourself out.*

6. *Your cat will be able to find his litter box—and stop using your pile of clothes.*

7. *Your mother-in-law will be able to stop in for an unexpected visit—and stay.*

8. *Your children will have to go outside to play jungle explorer.*

9. *You will be able to find your children and take their faces off the milk cartons.*

10. *You will no longer have an excuse for not having sex with your spouse. (Although if this is a problem, there are still headaches.)*

14 | Keep Clutter at Bay

"This is not the end. It is not even the beginning of the end.
But it is, perhaps, the end of the beginning."
—Winston Churchill

ooray! We did it. We got our clutter on the run. Now let's keep it that way. If we follow these daily habits, we will spend a lot less time on major cleanups and we will keep our lives and souls clutter-free. It will be hard at first, and we will not be able to do all of these things every day. Do what you can every day until it becomes a habit.

While practicing these habits, I found that I got bored, felt myself slipping into a rut. I even wondered if I had become obsessive about neatness! So I tried not to do any of these things. The next day, I didn't feel as good about myself. I let everything go for two days and felt that old, dark, depressed, clutter thinking return. I returned to my new habits, but it was a lot harder than keeping them up from the beginning. We will all have times when we just don't want to do these things. So we won't! There, we showed that clutter who was boss! This temporary declaration of independence is like canceling a check to a creditor—we pay far more later. For myself, I find that I am good about keeping the kitchen and bedroom in perfect order, but slack off in the other areas. Oh well, I am getting better. So are you.

Newspapers

I love newspapers. I used to write for them, so I have a special passion for them. But they are the enemy. Most people don't need to subscribe to more than one daily. Regardless, remember that they are *daily* papers. Read them that day and throw them away. There is nothing in them that is not available online, or in libraries. If you must save an article (and my advice is don't), clip it immediately (keep a pair of scissors next to where you read), file it immediately, and recycle the rest of the paper immediately.

Weeklies are fun. They have calendars and reviews of the weekend's events. Use the calendar and throw the thing away on Tuesday or Wednesday. Put the calendar on a bulletin board, throwing away last week's.

Mail

Open mail over a trash can or recycling bin. Immediately toss Ed McMahon. He will write you again. If it looks like it is junk, it probably is. Generally, you will toss 30 percent of incoming mail. Take what is left and deal with it. If it is a bill, put it in the "to be paid basket" immediately. Then follow the suggestions in Chapter 10. Set aside a time each evening to respond to personal mail and any business mail that you saved. File it or toss it when done. There is really no way to totally get off junk mail lists, as there are more than one. It will at least help to write to: Mail Preference Service, Direct Marketing Assn., P.O. Box 9008, Farmingdale, NY 11735-9008.

E-mail

Read, respond, delete. Be ruthless. I get hundreds of e-mails a day. Even if I saved them, I could not find them if I needed them. Set up a filing system in your e-mail program for those items that are worth saving. Don't just dump everything into "my e-mail" or "my documents." Take some time to organize several directories (see Chapter 15).

Dishes

Wash them at least once a day. It takes less time to wash them in the evening than it will if you let them go for a few days. I tried it and not only does it take more time, but you face a mess every time you go into your kitchen. This can set up feelings of being a failure and lead to a relapse of old behavior. If you make coffee in the morning, get it ready in the evening. I have to wash my espresso stuff and regular pot before I can put fresh grounds in them, and as long as I am at it, I use the soap and time to wash the rest of the dishes. Time spent: seven minutes. Peace of mind: enormous.

Yes, you can soak dishes to make them easier to clean, but my experiments showed that soaking for an hour did about as much good as two days.

Clothes

It's easy to leave the clean clothes in the laundry basket after washing—forever. Folding clothes is boring. If you can't fold them when you get them out of the dryer, do it in front of the TV. Same for ironing. I bought my first iron two years ago, and I found that ironing's not that bad. Hang up the ironed clothes right away.

Bed

If your read in bed, put the books on the floor and not on the bed. If you eat in bed, get up and put the dishes in the sink. These little habits will pay off big time. In the morning, making a bed without books or ice cream bowls in it is a lot easier. You don't have to make your bed military style, unless you are really recovered. Just pull the sheets and cover up over the pillows and it will look 100 times better. And your dog or cat will be happier, too.

Bathroom

If you keep a sponge by the tub, you can give it a quick wipe just before you get out and that nasty ring won't show up for a longer time. Give the faucets on the sink and tub a quick wipe with a dry towel before you leave. It will do wonders for your self-esteem when you come home from work. Time: negligible.

Living Room

Don't use that coffee table for a bookcase or filing cabinet. Put things where they belong. Newspapers love to mingle on coffee tables and sofas. Send them to a newspaper singles bar—the trash/recycle bin. They will be happier together. How much time does it take to pick up the evening's glasses and cups? About two minutes. Ashtrays are particularly gross. Dump 'em.

Dining Room

That was a really nice dinner you prepared in your clean kitchen. Now pick up the dishes, as you are going to wash them anyway. Wipe the table. Time: perhaps five minutes. If you live with someone else, they will generally be very happy to help with this chore. They are so happy at the progress you are making.

A Small Investment

We have spent about 15 or 20 minutes spread throughout our day to give ourselves a better life. That is a very small investment for a very big reward. If we let these things slide, we can look forward to losing a good couple of hours of our weekends doing the same things. Personally, I would rather be fishing. How about you?

15 | Your Computer: The Broken Promise

"Any sufficiently advanced technology is indistinguishable from magic."
—Arthur C. Clarke

Your computer reacts to clutter much as you do. It operates more slowly, can't seem to work right when it is full of useless files, and will crash if you don't declutter it. This chapter will teach you to get rid of the junk that slows your computer down and makes it work inefficiently. The first section briefly outlines computer decluttering basics for beginners, and the second section goes into greater detail for the more technologically adept.

The Short Version

Here is a quick trick that will get you started and reclaim some space right away. To really declutter your computer, read on, but if you just do this one thing, you will be better off than when you started. (Note: The specifics here apply to Windows 98, though much of the material will apply to Windows 95. "Me," the millennium edition of Windows, just came out, so I haven't delved into it yet.)

Weekly cleaning

Weekly, empty your recycle bin (the trashcan on your desktop). Right click on it. From the drop-down menu, choose "explore" and review the list of files. If there's nothing you want to save, click "file," and "empty recycle bin." If you see a file you want to save, highlight it, then click "restore."

Monthly cleaning

Run "disk cleanup" monthly. Go to programs/accessories/system tools/disk cleanup. This will show a lot of useless info, including Windows 98 uninstall info, the recycle bin, temporary files and more. It is almost always safe to use this utility. You can also uninstall a lot of Windows garbage, like wallpapers (called "backgrounds"), Web TV (if you don't have it), and so on by clicking on the "more options" tab, "windows components," and choosing the ones you don't need. Don't worry, if you delete one you need, you can always reinstall it from the Windows CD. After deleting what you want, reboot, try your programs, and if everything works, go back to accessories/system tools and run "scandisk." If everything checks out okay, run "disk defragmenter."

That's it! This is the safest and easiest way to get rid of a lot of junk. Now, onward for those who want to know more and do a thorough job.

For the Computer Literate and Techies

I got my first computer in 1982. Since then, I have been fascinated by them and have been a programmer and a power user. I used to believe computers would create the "paperless office," but I now realize that that is a broken promise. Still, computers can make our lives easier and less cluttered if we use them correctly.

All programs add clutter to your hard drives. "Readme" files that seldom contain useful information, "help" files that don't, useless graphics and "wav" files that are cute at first but then are just annoying all clog up your hard drive's arteries.

A short review of decluttering programs

Organizing and decluttering programs clutter store shelves. They all promise to eliminate useless clutter from your hard drive. They are all optimistic.

I own every decluttering program on the market. They all have failings. The "new and improved" versions promise to be better than the last buggy ones. Sometimes they are better, but often introduce new bugs. I've used programs by Quarterdeck, Symantec, Mace, Cybermedia, and others. Each has its own limitations. Each does some good. And each can corrupt your Windows operating system. The worst is Powercleaner. Avoid it! Cybermedia Uninstaller has proven to be the best for me. Norton (Symantec) is probably second best.

Find out what you have

Click "my computer" on your desktop. It will show your hard drives. Right-click them and you'll see a graphic representation of your disk capacity and free space. If you have less than 50 percent free space, you are heading for trouble. Windows needs plenty of disk space to make swap files. The more you have, the more it will use. (You can adjust this feature, but you shouldn't, unless you really know what you are doing). If the free space is too small, Windows will get choked up and periodically crash.

Back up

Before you use any decluttering program, back up your hard drives. Make a separate backup of your Windows files. Find your backup program or make a new bootable system floppy disk with your backup program so that it can access your backup tape or CD in case of disk failure. Label those bootable floppies and put them where you can find them with your trembling, sweaty hands if you get a "disk not formatted," or "hard disk failure" message.

Run an image file, which is a picture of your hard disks made by Norton, Mace, and other utility programs. In the event of a crash, you can use them to reconstruct your computer. Run it automatically at startup to be safe. It will cause a long delay in booting, but it is worth it. *Turn this option off* before you reboot after decluttering. *Do not* run it manually after you have finished deleting files. If you do, you will have an image of the damage you have just done. Wait until you are sure everything works. Fortunately, these programs make a .BAK image, which is the previous image.

Using Decluttering Programs

Turn on the decluttering program's "undo or unerase" feature. Tempting as it is, don't just wade in like John Wayne storming the beach at Iwo Jima and try to declutter your system in one sitting. Like you did when decluttering your rooms, work on one area at a time. Delete the "safe" files first. Reboot periodically and see if those files were really safe to delete. If they were, and everything operates smoothly, make another backup of your system files.

The safest files to eliminate are the .tmp, .wav, .gif, .avi, .mov, .pcx, .jpg, (also shown as .jpeg), readme, .wri, screensavers, wallpaper, and setup files (if you still have the original disks or CD-ROMs), as well as downloaded .exe files that you have already decompressed and used to update your programs. Be careful not to eliminate the .pcx or .jpg files that start up with programs. The programs get sulky if they can't give you an advertising message at startup. Bak files are generally safe, but for God's sake, don't get rid of system.bak, anything with .win in it, autoexec.bak, config.bak, or image.bak. Avoid messing with anything that starts with an underscore (_).

If you upgraded from Windows 3.1 to 95 or 98 (and I presume 2000 or "Me," but I haven't installed it yet), Windows saved a copy of the old operating system. If everything is working okay (or at least as well as Windows ever works), then get rid of it. It takes up 7 to 20 MB of space. One file in particular, data.z, seems to spread itself around quite a bit.

Even if Windows isn't working all that well, and it has been months or years since you upgraded, chances are the problems have nothing to do with the upgrade and it is safe to delete those files. You can always reinstall Windows, which can either be simple or only slightly less painful than a root canal. I have reinstalled Windows 98 several times because of corrupt files. Sometimes you have to reinstall programs to make them work afterwards, so make sure you have the CDs or disks for programs you want to use again. Make sure you have the installation keys or codes that came with the program or you might not be able to reinstall them. If you "borrowed" a program like Word, WordPerfect, any

Adobe programs, any Microsoft programs, and some others, you may have to get honest and get a new copy for yourself.

New versions

A word of warning about buying new versions. You save money by buying an upgrade, but, if you don't have the original program, you won't be able to install the upgrade. If you can afford it, get the full version. If you buy a "competitive upgrade," you should be able to install it, as long as you have one of the programs listed on the box.

Fonts, program files, DLLs

Fonts are *usually* safe to delete, but be careful. I've deleted fonts and found out that my word processing programs needed them. Calls to tech support solved the problem and the techies were familiar with the problem. It happens all the time.

Program files are the juiciest ones to go after, since they take up the most space. The danger is that, no matter how innocuous a program seems, it could be using an essential file that Windows needs. So backup, backup, backup.

Redundant .dll files can be troublesome. To get to these, use your uninstaller program's "spacemaker," "find duplicate files," or "clean up the registry" features. Although most of these files are useless, you could delete one crucial one that your uninstaller misread, and then Windows won't work, or it will give you that annoying message that a necessary .dll file is missing. "Hit any key" sometimes works, and sometimes it pushes you into "safe" mode. The way to find out what is causing the problem is to hit the F8 key (without the sledgehammer you want to use), upon booting and choose "Line by line confirmation." When you get to the line that has the file that caused the problem, hit "skip" and keep going. This will get you booted and you can reinstall the deleted program.

Cleaning Up Without a Decluttering Program

Even if you don't have one of the uninstaller programs, you can make great headway just by using Windows Explorer. Find the directory C:/windows/temp. This is a hoard of clutter. Nearly 100 percent of the time it is perfectly safe to slash and burn the files in it. However, nothing is safe all the time. I've had times where I've done nothing more than clean out the directory (that means eliminating the files, not the directory itself), and then found that some bizarre program wouldn't work afterwards. That is why you should never delete files from your recycle bin until you are absolutely sure that everything works properly.

The safest thing is to delete the files, which are put in your recycle bin, reboot, and try all your important programs. If all is well, after a few days of reboots using every program you have, you can empty the recycle bin. You don't get the advantage of freeing space until you have emptied your recycle bin. By the way, you can select the entire directory by highlighting the first file, holding down the shift key, and selecting the last file. Alternatively, you can hold down the control key and select individual files. This is true in any directory.

You can search for specific types of files by using the "find" feature in your "start" menu. Find "files or folders." A pop-up menu will appear asking if you want to find files "named _____." Type in the extension of the types of files you want to eliminate. For example, type "*.bmp" to find bitmap files, "*.bak" to root out backup files, and so on. Use the shift or control methods above to select the ones you want to send to computer heaven.

The Internet and Clutter

The Internet is a clutter hog. Many Web sites leave behind cookies that make it easier to go back to them, but they take up space. Both Internet Explorer and Netscape Navigator have features that claim to delete cookies, but they lie. They offer to clean your cache, and all offline content, but don't get half of them.

Using Windows Explorer, go to C:/windows/temporary Internet files. You will be aghast at the stuff in there. This directory is sneaky. Leave the files dated about three days from the last time you used the Internet. After you delete all the information, save it in your recycle bin. About 90 percent of the time, you will have no problems, but sometimes, the next time you try to load your browser, it won't work. If it doesn't, undelete those files from the recycle bin. If that doesn't work, you may have to reinstall Internet Explorer or Netscape, which are downloads. So only work on one browser at a time.

Besides taking up space, these files will allow anyone to track where you have been on the Internet. So, if you have accidentally browsed, say, "Ophelia's Forbidden Fantasies" and don't want your wife, girlfriend, boyfriend, or kids to know, empty that directory! The same holds true for your "history" or "favorites" lists. Periodically empty them.

Security

Just ask Monica Lewinsky how much good it does to delete files and old e-mails using Microsoft Explorer. Just because you can't see them doesn't mean that someone else can't resurrect them. To completely eliminate files from your system, you need to use a security erase from Norton or McAffee or other such programs.

Hidden junk

There is a sneaky directory that hides other Internet junk. It is C:/ windows/temporary Internet files/contentIE5 (or whatever version of Internet Explorer you are using). *Do not* delete the folders you find there. While it may be safe, you will get a Windows warning and I am afraid of those. Instead, go into each directory and delete the files you find. After you do this, you will find that your Web browser loads more slowly at first, but it soon makes the files it needs again. I have found that I have to connect and disconnect a couple of times to get everything back to normal. On the second reconnect, everything worked fine. But, just in case, don't delete the files from your recycle bin until you are sure everything works again. With computers, a just-in-case attitude makes good sense.

Clean out your "history" folder in Netscape (under communicator/tools). Again, leave the last three days info to be safe. Another thing you can do to cut down the clutter is to delete the *.fat file from your browser. Your browser will have to rebuild it, but it's not a big deal. You have to go to the directory where your browser is. It is under programs.

Finally, Something Truly Safe To Delete!

All graphics, desktop publishing, and word processing programs come with clip art. Lots of it. Most of the time, you don't need or use it. This is a perfectly safe area to use your machete. If you are really into desktop publishing, you probably have extra clip art that has from half a million to more than one million images. Fortunately, the better programs leave it on the CD-ROM and let you pick and choose. So far so good. But, after you have made that wonderful newsletter or publication, the embedded art stays on your hard drive. I used to publish a newsletter using lots of clip art. A year later, when the newsletter was useless, the clip art was still hogging space.

Backup the publication onto a CD-ROM or tape drive in a special directory and get rid of the original. Chances are you will never need it again, but if you do, you can find it. If you download Web pages or photos, they are chock-full of garbage. Feel perfectly safe in deleting ".spacer" and ".gif " files where you store the downloaded pages. Using a photo editor, preview those files. If Aunt Tillie e-mailed you pictures of the grandchildren, you can cut them down to size. Most people don't compress e-mail images. Convert them to .jpg images if they are in .bmp format. Then you can safely compress them by at least 30 percent before degradation sets in. It's not an exact science. Make a copy and then view it next to the original. If it still looks good to you compressed, then delete the original. I design Web pages and some files can compress to eight to 10 KB and look good and others can't go below 50 KB. Experiment.

A Clean Desktop Is a Godly Desktop

The desktop is a handy place to put shortcuts for programs you use frequently. Computer manufacturers clutter it up with shortcuts to programs that are useless. Hewlett Packard and others place an update icon there. You don't need it. The feature is in your "HP Utilities" directory (or whatever your manufacturer names it). Since many clutterers like to visually organize things, fearing that they will lose them if they file them, they put a lot of shortcuts on their desktops. Then, when these favorite programs are replaced by other favorite programs, we don't delete the old shortcut. These are absolutely safe to delete. The program is still in your start menu, so if you really need it, you can still run it. Right-click the shortcut and it will tell you where the program is supposed to be. Go there, verify that, and make sure an icon in your "programs" menu leads to it. If it doesn't, cut the one from the desktop and paste it into the "Programs" menu. I'll tell you how to organize this overstuffed menu later.

TSRs (Take Up Space Ridiculously)

TSRs (Terminate and Stay Resident) programs load themselves into your base memory on startup. All you really need are: Explorer, Systray and your anti-virus program (Navapw32 for Norton). But there may be a weird one that has made itself indispensable. When you close apparently "useless" programs, sometimes it will have unexpected results. If you are running a network, chances are that it has inserted some program into memory, so don't mess with that one. Rnaapp is used by Microsoft Networking and should be left alone. As always, have a startup disk handy so that if things don't work, you can go back and undo your changes. If you use MSN and Hotmail, they insert "msmgs" to notify you of new e-mail. I find this annoying, so I disable it.

So how do you get rid of these pesky, RAM-stealing hogs? Go to programs/accessories/system tools. The first screen will tell you how much ram you have installed and how much is free. You might be shocked. With no programs running, even with a network, you should have between 90 and 96 percent of your system resources free. When I first checked, I had only 82 percent free, which was causing my programs to lock up and act erratically. This base RAM is not affected by how much memory you have on your system. It is limited to 640K. More RAM will help programs run better and may solve some problems, but has nothing to do with this.

The Real Startup Menu

Go to the tools tab under the system configuration utility option. This is the real startup menu. (Forget that cute one under Programs.) When I looked here I found programs loading for a printer that had gone to printer heaven years ago, a bill-minder program that I ignored even when I used it, and many others. My favorite was one called, "Time Sink Ad Gateway." This sneaky devil had been inserted into my startup by some nefarious Web site designer so that I would always be able to see his ads!

My Internet service provider had put a cute little menu on my taskbar that ate up RAM. I could access it from the desktop anyway, so didn't see the point of having both. Oil Change (a useless program) had inserted itself into my startup. Norton had inserted its Cleansweep checker, even though I had disabled that program from the suite.

Expand the menu box so that you can see the directories where these programs live, to make sure you don't mess with anything that resides in Windows or Windows/system. All you have to have is System Tray, ScanRegistry, LoadPowerProfile (rundll.exe), Rnaapp, and your virus checker. Uncheck everything else, then click apply and okay. Your system will have to reboot for the changes to take effect. Microsoft Office Startup keeps rechecking itself, so just give up on that one.

Success!

Once you have finished this process, your computer should be happier and your toolbar will be gloriously uncluttered. Most importantly, you will have taken control and the computer will be your slave instead of your master.

Good Stuff

If you use Microsoft Word, you will find a clutter trove and time-saver under tools/AutoCorrect. (WordPerfect has a similar spot, but I abandoned that star-crossed program years ago, so you'll have to find the similar option yourself.) Here you'll find words that are automatically inserted or corrected as you type. There is a lot of garbage in there, but the neat thing is that you can insert an AutoCorrect feature for words you commonly mistype. I tend to type mediation instead of meditation, and as I communicate with my Higher Power more often than with recalcitrant parties, it made sense to correct it. In order to type mediation, I had to go in and delete the word from the list. As soon as I finished typing this paragraph, I reinserted meditation for mediation. You are not stuck with a choice if you need to fix it, or if you misspell the word you want in the first place.

Start Menu

To unclutter your Start menu, make file folders with big concepts, such as "publishing programs," "Internet," "business," "finance," "utilities," and the like. One way to do this is to create the folder on your desktop, copy it, open "Programs," and paste it anywhere. Then drag the folder for, say, Quicken, to the new folder named "finance." Quicken will now be under "finance." If you have a lot of business programs, make subfolders for specific needs. When you are done, you will have a clean Start menu that reflects the way you think and work and not the way a thousand egotistical program manufacturers think you should work.

Final Notes

Please, please, don't put all your documents under "my documents." Putting them all there is like filing everything in a filing cabinet under "A." After a while, you won't be able to find anything. Set up a filing system.

Run Scan Disk and Disk Defragmenter at least once a month. Delete e-mails as you read them. See Chapter 16 for detailed advice about scanners, faxes, and other devices that I believe fail to live up to their promises.

16 | The Home Office

"The birth of excellence begins with out awareness that our beliefs are a choice."
—Tony Robbins

H ave the following thoughts ever crossed your mind, or even been said to you by "friends"?

"How can a clutterer run a business? You need the structure of an office run by a tyrant! You are so disorganized that you will fail." If so, take the advice of my mother, who said, "People will tell you 10 reasons why you can't do something. Ignore them."

We can do anything we want to do. We have to change some beliefs and patterns of behavior, but that's what this book is all about. If you already have your own business and are overwhelmed by your cluttering, you can change that. If you are afraid to get out of a job you hate because of your cluttering, you can change that. Yes, it is tough to run a business, even for organized people. But we clutterers have an advantage that logical thinkers don't. We are inventive. We are able to devise all sorts of strategies to circumvent our disorder. We have the creativity to see things differently. If we are recovering, we can turn our greatest liability into our greatest asset. As Einstein said, "Imagination is more important than knowledge."

Admitting the Need for Change Is Not Admitting Defeat

Clutterers can be successful in any business they choose, if they choose to recover. I've run two businesses at one time even while I was in the midst of my depression and clutter. One of them was successful and the other, I finally realized, was a money-loser. As I came out of my clutter fog, I tossed one of the businesses. Having a losing business didn't make me a loser. I was as much of a success as I could be at the time. Dumping it was a statement of belief in myself— that I deserved more reward for my time.

So, here is what I have done, now that I have recovered somewhat, to make a business work.

How to Make It Work

Walk into your home office and look at it with fresh eyes. Oh boy, oh boy. You *need* all the stuff here, right? Wrong. I got ruthless with my home office when I moved. I went through all my "necessary" stuff again when I moved up to a real office. Rather than cart a lot of useless files, I went through them. Year-old information requests seemed valuable, because I thought I could use them for a mailing list. Then I thought about it. If I hadn't made a mailing list yet, what were the chances that I would do so in the near future? I chose to eliminate the clutter to let new business flow in. And guess what—it did.

Our home office is our expression of our confident, prosperous self. It should inspire confidence in ourselves, even if we never receive clients. For years, I lived in fear that one of my suppliers would want to visit my office. In fact, I lost a big contract because one wanted to see my operation. There is no stigma attached to working out of a home office anymore. However, a disorganized office will send people running. It is easy to make mistakes in a disorganized office. It is easy to waste inordinate amounts of time in a disorganized office. Declutter and you will have all sorts of time to grow your business. You will also feel more like an executive, which is what you are. You are the president, CEO, and SFO, so act like it!

Goals

Prosperity thinkers will have goals written down and taped to the walls, along with positive sayings. I have "Seven Steps to a Prosperity Consciousness," an anonymous piece given to me years ago in a church I no longer remember, taped beside my computer. Periodically, I write, "Today, I will create 10 new deals." There is nothing mystical or impractical about this. When I was a direct salesman, even the most unspiritual, greedy, economic successes that I knew used these techniques. Og Mandingo, who is revered by sales managers as a motivational god, stated, "The Second Commandment of Success: Thou must learn with patience ye can control thy destiny."

There are dozens of books on running an efficient office. Go ahead and get one or two. Once you get past the clutter mentality and apply these principles, you will benefit from them. While most of the information is just plain common sense, these few suggestions will help clutterers deal with their special situations.

Keeping It Together

Information keeps flowing in. There are faxes to read, faxes to send, brochures to create, file, and mail, mail to be opened, bills to pay and send out. Once we learn to put everything in its place and deal with things as they come up, we can be efficient. Once we have decluttered and made space for success, we will want to keep it that way.

Filing cabinets

How many filing cabinets do you have? If the answer is more than four, you are either very successful or a clutterer. If you can actually get into them, and the files are not smashed up against each other, you are probably in pretty good shape.

The key is to organize things so that you can find them. Simple, huh? Clutterers do best when they put things into "big pictures," since our tendency is to get bogged down in minutiae. Don't bother with color-coding systems, subsystems, and other complicated systems. Clutterers need to keep it simple. Like with like.

I've found that different cabinets for different aspects of my work make it easier. When I was writing a lot about Mexico, I had a whole cabinet devoted to this subject. Now it is one drawer. When I was promoting my "Mexico Mike" persona, I had two drawers of clips and ideas. Now that he is history, I tossed a few hundred copies of newspaper stories about him, keeping a dozen or so of each. Sure, it was great to have the clipping of me on the front page of the *Wall Street Journal* or the full-page spread in the *New York Times*, but I no longer send them out, so I don't need a hundred of each. Reviews of my previous 10 books are nice to keep for memories, but *Mexico From the Driver's Seat, Mexico's Colonial Heart,* and so on are out-of-print, so why keep several copies? If I ever need one, I can photocopy it.

Now my spa reservation business is paramount. It occupies an entire four-drawer cabinet. Spas themselves take two drawers and customers take another. The fourth is for expansion. Allow for expansion, but not clutter. The main category is spa business, and it is subdivided from there. But I keep the subdivisions as simple as possible.

If you can't get to your files, they are useless. A lot of wasted space is usually taken up by too many dividing hanging files and manila folders. You need a hanging file for each letter of the alphabet to hold miscellaneous information, but you don't need a manila folder for each bit of info if it is not something you refer to a lot. Don't crowd the hanging files. Make two or more hangers for a subject if it has a lot of manilas in it. And if you are saving a newspaper clipping, clip it! Don't save the whole page.

Computer manuals/registration numbers

Clutterers tend to buy programs, install them, and toss the CDs and registration forms into a pile. We really have to take care of these things right away, or we won't take care of them at all. I file the registration numbers in a hanging folder marked, "computer," with a subfolder called "registration numbers." That's it! Sure, you could subfile by type of program, but these are one-page items and shouldn't take up that much space. File these right away!

The manuals should be accessible in a bookshelf where nothing else lives. Write the registration numbers on the flyleaf for those awful times when you need to call tech support. If you do this, you may never have to refer to your paper file, but redundancy here is worthwhile.

CDs/floppy disks

As a clutterer, I wasted lots of time looking for lost CDs. Today I use a lazy-susan-type slotted tower for CDs. There are four sides to it and each side is a particular type of program: "Utilities," "Drivers," and "Modem/Phone" live in one tower, with space for expansion. "Business," "Graphics/Photo," etc. live in another. Remember "like with like"? I've never found a really good floppy organizer, but use the same principles.

Pens, tape, scissors, paperclips, etc.

All these live in one place, with a separate set for my partner. Extra pens and scissors live by the fax machine.

Deal With It, File It, Toss It

When a fax comes in, try to deal with it immediately, make a decision, and file it. Not all faxes need to be kept. Throw away ones that are not really necessary. A wastebasket should be your most used filing system.

Phone messages need to be dealt with. If it's a one-time call, toss number right away. Otherwise enter it into your database and toss the note.

The mail needs to be read daily. Most of it should be tossed. Open it over a trash or recycling can. Unless you are truly interested in an advertisement, dump it. This will save you tons of time in deciding what to do with it. Bills should be put in a "bills to be paid" file, which should be looked at once a week and dealt with. Suze Orman recommends writing the checks right away and putting them into their envelopes in order to get them out of the way (see Chapter 10).

Time Clutter

Clutterers have trouble with clock time. It is just too easy to imagine that we have all the time in the world to complete projects. A simple project manager program enables you to define a goal, break it down into major tasks, and further subdivide it into individual subtasks to accomplish those goals. For example, my goal was "write a book," the major tasks I had to do were "research" and "writing," and the subtasks included "write introduction," "interview experts," "write Chapter 1," "write Chapter 2," and so on.

Get Visual

I know a clutterer who is a very successful businessman. He knows that his tendency is to "file and forget," so, being visually oriented, he had cubbyholes built behind his desk so he could see the messages and projects he needed to attend to. A big calendar on the wall (one with plenty of space to write on) is a good visual reminder. A corkboard is a great visual reminder, as long as you are ruthless about weeding it. Clear it out once a week.

E-mail

We want to keep it all! Don't. Reply, leaving the original message attached, add the person to your address book, and delete the original. The copy is still there in your "sent" file.

Scanning Documents

Everybody asks me about this as a way to cut down on clutter. It *could* work, in theory. I've used scanners since 1990. I've just never been able to find a way to make them work right. It does make sense to scan articles and letters into OCR (optical character recognition) files in your word processor. However, scanning is not a cure-all for paper clutter, because it becomes too easy to scan everything—even useless items. The only difference between storing junk on your computer and in your paper files is that it doesn't take up as much room in your house. When you intelligently decide what needs to be saved and what needs to be pitched, then a scanner can work for you. The OCR programs have improved and can read most documents pretty well. If you have an intelligently organized filing system on your computer, these could be a good way to cut down on paper clutter. But remember, hard drives crash. If you don't have a backup tape or CD, those important documents could be lost forever.

Computer Faxing

Technophile that I am, I jumped on this! For a time I got faxes directly into my computer. The problem here was that not all fax machines could interact with it. And there were those times when a client (particularly from Mexico) called to ask for a fax tone. Somehow the transmission never got through.

Then I discovered Efax. This is a system (and there are other companies that do this) that has all your faxes routed to them and then they send it to you via e-mail. It worked pretty well, until I started getting more junk faxes than real faxes. Another problem was that the handwriting on faxes was illegible. I did find it useful as a backup when I was on the road and was able to get my faxes on my laptop. There is a monthly fee for using this service.

I have a friend who runs a publishing business and he relies solely on the above system. He doesn't even own a fax machine and it saves him from having to have a second or third phone line. Unfortunately, in order to send a fax, he has to scan the document, then e-mail it, which causes the resolution to deteriorate.

Personally, I gave up. I use a real fax machine and pay for a second line. Call me old fashioned.

In Brief

KISS—Keep it simple, success!

17 | Notable Hoarders

On April 14, 2000, Phillip Katz died at the age of 37. He was the founder of PK-Ware and author of PKZIP/PKUNZIP software. Although he was a millionaire, his condo in an exclusive suburb of Milwaukee was, according to an Associated Press story on April 20, 2000, knee deep in garbage and decaying food. The city had to clean up "debris several feet thick," including partially eaten fast-food meals. The refuse filled two 20-cubic-yard trash containers. "Several fly strips were hanging in the kitchen, and they were totally black from flies and gnats. Numerous mouse droppings were observed throughout the scattered garbage and rubbish."

Neighbors had been calling the health department years before he died because of the stench coming from his house and the presence of rodents and insects. The city had come in and cleaned up, sending Mr. Katz a bill and a fine. He never responded. He was no longer living in his home, but rather residing in a series of cheap hotels near the strip joints he frequented.

Mr. Katz left the following phone message at the offices of the *Milwaukee Journal-Sentinel*: "I've been kind, nice, and generous to people in my life. I'm not an evil person. If you want to go ahead and destroy my reputation, I suppose that's your prerogative. There are a lot worse people in the world than myself. I don't know why you're doing this to me." A city health official said, "It doesn't appear that Mr. Katz's problems are related to money. His difficulty is in some other realm."

Katz had built a software empire, but didn't like running it. He stayed away from the office for weeks at a time, living in cheap hotels and going to strip clubs. According to a dancer who says she was a good friend of his, Katz was shy and always ready to help people. She said he was taken advantage of by some people, but he was so lonely that he was grateful for anyone who considered him a friend.

Katz had other problems as well; he died alone in a cheap hotel from pancreatic bleeding as a result of acute alcoholism.

The Strange Saga of the Collyer Brothers

The Collyer brothers, Homer and Langley, were notorious recluses and hoarders. They were born into one of the best, wealthiest families in New York City in the 1880s. They lived with their mother in a luxurious mansion in Harlem in the early 1900s. As the neighborhood declined around them, they booby-trapped the house and boarded up the windows to keep potential intruders out. They turned off the water, electricity, and gas in the mansion, using only a small kerosene heater.

Homer became blind and eventually paralyzed, so Langley took care of him. In 1942, when their bank attempted to foreclose on their mortgage, the police could not get in because of the wall of newspapers and other junk erected as a barricade. Langley simply wrote out a check for the full mortgage. He explained the collection of newspapers to a reporter from the New York *Herald Tribune* as follows: "I am saving newspapers for Homer, so that when he regains his sight he can catch up on the news."

They were left alone until March 21, 1947, when a neighbor told the police that there was a dead body in their house. A policeman went to investigate, but he couldn't get in. A squad of patrolmen was called in and broke the door down. However, they still couldn't get in, because they were met with a wall of junk: old newspapers, chairs, boxes, a sewing machine, and other strange debris.

The cops tried the second-story window. There they encountered more newspapers, boxes, and assorted junk. When they cleared a path, they found Homer dead on the floor. His hair was down to his shoulders and he wore only a ragged bathrobe. Brother Langley was nowhere to be found. *The New York Times* chronicled the removal of junk from their house and the search for the missing body for 18 days, from March 21, 1947, to April 8, 1947.

A few days after they found Homer, the police searched the house and discovered mountains of junk, a car body, the top of a horse-drawn carriage, and six tons of newspapers. The next day, they found more refuse, but no brother. The next day, besides junk, they found bankbooks with deposits of over $3,000.

During the second week, 3,000 books, lots of phone books, a Steinway piano, an X-ray machine, and a horse's jawbone were excavated. Of course, there were more newspapers. So far, 19 tons of useless items had been removed. By the end of the saga, 103 *tons* of clutter and garbage were taken from the house.

Langley was found dead about 10 feet away from the first body, being chewed on by a rat, covered by newspapers, a suitcase, and other debris. He had been asphyxiated by his junk when one of his booby traps fell on him. Police theorize that he was burrowing through the maze of garbage to bring food to his brother, when the tunnel collapsed. Brother Homer had died of starvation.

An English Eccentric

An English woman who died in 1866 had refused to allow anyone into her mansion for years following her husband's death. When the authorities entered, the smell of rotting garbage was overwhelming. Though very wealthy, she slept on a rotting hair mattress and wore only one dress. Her house was so cluttered with garbage that there was only a small path to walk from the door to the other rooms. The hallway contained several statues, some of which were 8 feet tall, but they were hidden from sight by piles of books and bags of garbage. Five tons of books were removed from the house. Then the searchers found sacks upon sacks of perfectly new, unused items that had never been opened, but carried home from the shops and deposited wherever there was a space.

It may help hoarders to know that they are not really alone or unique. I remember when I was diagnosed with epilepsy how grateful I was to find out that some of my literary heroes were epileptics. Rembrandt was a hoarder, collecting wooden cabinets of objects he used in paintings. Freud's famous statue collection may have been a sign of hoarding. Madame de Montespan, Louis XIV's mistress, was the first documented person to buy everything she saw. Sherlock Holmes, who was highly logical and yet kept his rooms in disarray and his tobacco in a Persian slipper, showed signs of hoarding. Andy Warhol was apparently a clutterer or hoarder. Einstein was a hoarder. And Howard Hughes added the hoarding of certain items to his other unusual behaviors.

18 | Hoarding and Community Health

"We are creating hope by the minute. One of the things I love about my job is that we are creating hope. It is one of the most satisfying jobs next to being to a mom."

—Linda Durham, professional organizer

We have all read stories in the newspapers about elderly people who, though they may have been wealthy, lived in filthy houses. We all hope that our mothers and fathers never end up that way, and we are sure that we won't. But the problem is not just the elderly. Hoarders of all ages can live in unsanitary conditions that threaten their lives. Hoarders and absentee landlords can also create conditions that threaten the public health and safety. When these conditions are present, code enforcement officers, compliance officers, zoning enforcement officers, police, and social workers can be called in. Police are particularly concerned about abandoned cars, empty lots, and abandoned buildings, which contribute to crime in a community. And all of the aforementioned types of clutter bring down property value. So in a sense, hoarding harms the health of the people and the community they live in.

Earlier, I mentioned a *Wall Street Journal* article from January 26, 1999, about Gretna, Louisiana. After reading the article, I spoke with the mayor of Gretna, the Honorable Ronnie C. Harris. The article mentioned that some residents were upset because they could no longer store their boats in their front yards. This was brought on by the enforcement of zoning regulations. The zoning regulations went into effect in 1989, but hadn't been rigorously enforced. You may think it is a long leap from cluttering to boats in the yard, but the regulations emphasize the wide-ranging effects of different kinds of clutter. Clutterers think they affect only themselves, but in fact their behavior spills out into their communities.

Gretna, founded in 1836, has had a long history of being independent from the nearby city of New Orleans. It has a unique atmosphere that many residents relish. I lived there several years ago and felt the difference between it and the Big Easy. But, as communities grow, they have to adapt to the times. Mayor Harris ran on a platform of cleaning up Gretna. Enforcing zoning was one way to do that. The old practice of parking one's boat in the front yard posed a health hazard and held down property value. The boats collected water, which bred mosquitoes and harbored rats and wildlife. So, in the interest of the community health and improving property values, the city started enforcing the zoning regulations that stated boats could only be parked on the sides of houses, where, presumably, the residents would take better care of them.

Police dislike abandoned vehicles because they provide a convenient storage area for drug dealers. Also, when a cruiser stops a potential dealer, he can throw his stash into the nearest boat or car and the police cannot search it.

Abandoned houses are another sore spot for law enforcement officers. They are used as dope hideouts and places for other crimes to take place. In the past five years, Gretna has torn down 40 to 50 blighted houses. When I asked Mayor Harris if this cut down on crime, he answered, "Absolutely. People want less government in their lives but want less crime." The elimination of the houses has caused "another 80 houses to clean up and repair. We get all the blight out of it. When we go in and tear them down, property values go up. Soar. When you remove blight it puts pressure on existing houses. This puts pressure on rental houses."

The end result? "The livability of the community is improved," Harris says. "People want to live here, feel it is safer community. It is more vibrant."

Junk cars are also a health hazard, and they are not limited to poorer neighborhoods (just as hoarders are not limited to any one socioeconomic level). Many otherwise neat people think nothing of holding on to a car that stopped running when Nixon did. According to Bobby Perez, a planning and community compliance officer in Galveston, Texas, junk cars attract all kinds of vermin. "Dogs, cats, opossums live in them until they eat all they can and then go into houses," he says. "They also are convenient breeding grounds for flies and roaches."

When a neighbor complains to the city about a house that smells, Perez goes to investigate. Generally, he can just tell the people living there to clean it up. If the occupants won't allow him into the house, he has to get a search warrant and call the health department. When the residents are elderly, he tries to get the family involved. "They are usually very cooperative," he observes. If there is no family, he says, "I often take it on myself to help the elderly. Then I will call the churches. We try to lead them on the right path for assistance. It usually works. The family is the first line of defense. The elderly are often too proud to ask for help. We try to help."

Perhaps the easiest first step in decluttering is to get rid of an excess vehicle. Most cities have arrangements with towing companies that will take it away. Many charities will come and get it for you and give you a tax deduction. Not only will you be doing yourself a favor, but you will be helping your community.

19 | Our Cluttered World

C luttering isn't limited to people's houses. On January 26, 1999, *The Wall Street Journal* reported that one of my old hometowns, Gretna, Louisiana , was in the running for the clutter capitol of the United States. Governor Huey Long's promise of "a chicken in every pot" had been modernized to "a boat in every yard." It seems that longtime residents didn't see anything wrong with having boats in their yards or cars that didn't run. A new city government took issue with it and ordered them to clean up.

According to a *Savannah Daily News* story a few years ago, Savannah, Georgia, had a serious problem with clutter. People's yards were filled garbage and adorned with abandoned cars. Vacant lots were either filled with tall grass or piles of wood, glass, and other debris. Now such cluttering is a violation of the town's nuisance ordinance. Property owners can be fined $100, plus $100 for each day the cleanup does not happen.

Space Clutter

In a November 4, 1997 article for *TechMall*, an online newsletter devoted to technological news, Jeffrey Dunsavage wrote that, "a 500-pound piece of debris passed within 1.5 miles of a satellite worth tens of millions of dollars," which was the Russian space station Mir. That same year, he reported, "a bit of debris the size of a paint fleck collided with the space shuttle Discovery, punching halfway through its windshield. Several months before that, a French-made Cerise satellite collided with a discarded rocket body and was destroyed. This was the first insured loss of an in-orbit satellite caused by orbital debris. But with the private launch industry growing and the number of satellites in low-Earth orbit increasing, it is unlikely to be the last."

Shipshape?

The first mate of a certain ship, who wishes to remain anonymous, told me that the term "shipshape" is inaccurate, at least on commercial ships. Although things may look orderly on a ship, every crew member has lockers crammed with junk. While attempting to clean out the junk from one ship he was on, he asked crewmen what a certain bulky piece of junk was used for. No one could tell him, but everyone resisted his attempts to get rid of it.

On a trip to Albania, the ship had picked up a lot of lumber in Peru, used to shore up the cargo in the hold. The ship's officers figured they could sell the lumber in Albania or trade it for something useful. The Albanian merchant who was to trade with them said he really didn't want the lumber, but would take it off their hands. "No way," the crew said. "We'll find a use for it." On the return trip, every crew member started some sort of building project. The wackiest was a hot tub. Building a hot tub from odd scraps of wood is a difficult project at best. Each crewman stuffed his locker with odd scraps of wood, refusing to throw them away, "in case they came in handy." The ship returned home with a lot of unfinished woodworking projects and half a hot tub.

Belize

An American friend of mine was excited when she heard that there was to be a Mennonite auction while she was living in Belize. She figured there would be a lot of undiscovered antiques squirreled away by the Mennonites. A Belizian woman brought her down to earth. "An antique in Belize is an old American stove," she said.

Belizians have a difficult time discarding old junk, as they would have to haul it somewhere "far away" (nobody seems to know exactly how far or exactly where the dump was) to get rid of it. So the junk sits around on their property, or is rolled to a nearby creek bed. One man's junk is another man's treasure, and natives often barter and exchange junk from one farm to another.

Mennonites are true believers in the adage, "waste not, want not," and often hold auctions that attract people from miles around. They auction off such valuable items as sacks of rusty, bent nails and tangles of used baling wire.

One successful Belizian junk collector would put Fred Sanford to shame. He buys junk by the ship container load. He has a cousin in Arkansas who collects items like non-working stoves and refrigerators, broken toilets, baling wire, and seized engine blocks, and ships them to him. In a way, it's recycling—Arkansas gets uncluttered, but Belize gets more cluttered.

Mexico

Old cars in Mexico are honored, much like cattle in India. No matter how old a Chevy is, it will stand in someone's yard as a tribute to the belief that anything can be fixed. The Mennonites are just as successful with their auctions here as in Belize.

Ever wonder where those old clothes you donated to Goodwill go? Most of them are packed into bundles like cotton, or left in garbage bags and shipped to border towns like McAllen, Texas. There, during the winter, they are pawed through by retirees looking for treasures. Most of them are shipped to Mexico or Belize, where they are sold. Now that's recycling in action!

20 | Professional Organizers

"An organizer knows you better than your spouse or mother. We know everything there is about you. We know your finances, your hiding places. You really need to know your organizer."

—Diane Snow, professional organizer

hile many of us are able to get our clutter under control through the help of other clutterers and increased self-awareness, a professional organizer has some distinct advantages. As I stated earlier, an organizer is detached, has seen it all, and does not judge. Earlier in the book, I stated that they could be tough, but that is not entirely fair. Most are compassionate people, but sometimes they have to be tough. Because of the emotional attachment we clutterers have to our stuff, some of us may have a hard time with that. My encounters with professional organizers whom I considered toughmay just have been the result of our personalities clashing. This is a good lesson in taking the time to find someone you can work with.

Consultations with professional organizers are confidential. Organizers will also be able to suggest new habits and systems to keep clutter from coming back. Their fees range nationwide from $35 to $150 an hour, with $40 to $50 being the mean. The range of fees depends on the experience of the organizer and the type of job she will tackle. (I use the pronoun "she," as most organizers seem to be women.) Many people will turn to an organizer when their own attempts to declutter and stay decluttered have not borne fruit.

Organizers may be especially helpful in the workplace, and some specialize in this area. Organizers specializing in time management and clutter control for companies are on the higher end of the pay scale. The next chapter is devoted specifically to clutter in the workplace and how to deal with it. This one deals with the efficacy of professional organizers in the personal arena.

What Is a Professional Organizer?

A "professional" organizer is someone who has made it her business to declutter others. While there is an organization of professional organizers, called the National Association of Professional Organizers, (P.O. Box 140647, Austin, TX 78714; 512-206-0151, fax 512-454-3036; *www.napo.net*), or NAPO, as it is abbreviated, members readily admit that there is, at present, no licensing in any state. NAPO was founded in 1985 and has 1,200 members worldwide. Members agree to operate by certain guidelines and respect the confidentiality of their clients. NAPO provides continuing education for members.

People who become organizers come from different fields. Many were once executive secretaries, corporate trainers, counselors, or corporate managers before being drawn into the profession. The business of professional organizers is growing rapidly. In Chicago alone, the membership in NAPO has doubled from 22 members in 1998-1999 to 44 in 1999-2000. Eight years ago there were only 18 members. Nationally,

NAPO has grown to 1,200 members, after starting with five only 15 years ago.

Oddly enough, another growth industry related to cluttering has been that of the self-storage industry! According to the Self-Storage Industry Web page (*www.selfstorage.org*), from 1997 to 1999, "the industry witnessed unparalleled sales and refinancing activity." In 1999, approximately 1,000 new self-storage facilities were built, adding to the 25,000 already operating. This is a 4 percent annual growth rate.

The stuff we store cannot be worth what it costs to keep. An organizer's client kept two storage units for two years, paying several hundred dollars so that "the kids would have it." When she died, the children sold what they could and threw away the rest.

Some professional organizers are generalists and some have chosen to concentrate on specific areas of expertise. For instance, Diane Snow of Arrange From A-Z in Chicago (773-202-9297, e-mail: *Arrangez@interaccess.com.*), used to specialize in hoarders, but now works exclusively with her passions of kitchens and closets and more space planning. "Everyone should work with their passion," she says. "One of the things that I don't work with is paper. I will not touch a piece of paper anymore. You need to do what you do best and when you do that, it shows." Snow has been a professional organizer for eight years.

Snow is a straightforward, witty, dynamic woman. One trusts her immediately. Like most organizers, she came to the business from the corporate arena. She used to be an executive secretary. "After I organized a company I would leave," she recalls. "It wasn't until 20 years later that it dawned on me that [organizing] was what I did. My husband heard about organizing businesses. A light bulb went off. That's what I am. I have always been meticulous. Blindfold me and I can find anything."

Like many organizers, Snow experienced cluttering in her family. "I came from a chaotic family. A grandmother who saved papers. When we cleaned up, we found papers from 1898. One of my aunts was meticulous. The other enjoyed shopping for bargains. She liked little collectibles. Her house was clean but there was something on everything."

"Mom loves to buy in bulk even though she lives in a small place. Grandmother and great-aunt had bathtubs that were full of stuff. Twice in my lifetime they were totally decluttered. While they were away the family decluttered their house. It improved their lifestyle. We were able to come as a family for the holidays. That *had* to feel good."

Families who don't have the time or have not been successful in helping their elderly relatives are likely to turn to professional organizers. There may be resistance from the hoarder to let a stranger into the house, and it will take some concerted effort to convince the loved one to accept the help. In many cases, the help will be successful, in the sense that the relative's environment is changed and they may want to keep it that way. But it will take time and repeated visits to change old habits.

Money and Emotional Factors

Money becomes an issue before a project can get done. For example, Snow told me of a time it took three hours to clean off an organ. "You couldn't even get to it. The clients had to read each and every piece of paper. Even junk mail." Obviously, at that rate, it would cost a fortune to declutter someone's house. If someone is going to hire an organizer, they should be ready to let the organizer do her job—or be ready to pay for a lot of her time.

Professional organizers are like members of any other industry. Some will consult with you for free. Some will charge an assessment fee. Some will deduct that from the work. Most work on an hourly basis. In New York, fees start at $75 and up. Most new organizers start at $35-50 an hour.

Is there any way to tell in advance what an organizer will cost? Some say no. Others say yes. My experience was that I encountered ones who gave a very broad range of the number of hours needed. Very few organizers will agree to do a job for a flat fee. Snow gave this example: "I just did a kitchen and it took 36 hours. I would say that three hours was the least time I spent in a kitchen. Everything was labeled and containerized on the 36 hour job. If I hadn't done that, it still would have taken 24. I make your kitchen functional. Every one of my clients has said, 'This makes sense.' I make sense out of your kitchen. I make it functional."

Emotions are another issue that makes it difficult to gauge how long a job will take. A team would be great, but there is often little room in the house for two people, much less a team. One great hindrance to someone accepting help from an outsider is humiliation. They are ashamed of the way they live and don't want anyone to know. Like the people ignoring the elephant in the living room, many clutterers think that not admitting their problem will make it go away. There is an old 12-step catchphrase that applies here: "Denial is not a river in Egypt." Once the organizer and the client have worked through the denial and the shame, they often have to deal with the emotional attachment that the hoarder has to all the things he has collected.

What an Organizer Can Do for You

As an outsider, with no emotional involvement in your stuff, an organizer can offer suggestions on what is worth keeping and what is not. She will know something about time management and efficiency and be able to suggest ways to organize things so that they won't get back into the disarray they were when she started.

Some organizers will also take on the responsibilities of a personal assistant, paying bills and setting you up on a schedule. For busy professionals, for whom time is an even more valuable commodity than money, such organizers can be a godsend. Both organizers and executive trainers I spoke with pointed out the benefits to busy people who travel a lot of having someone arrange for all the mundane jobs, such as getting the grass cut, the laundry done, and the car serviced.

Lynn Meyer, owner of All About Time in Chicago (312-222-1856; *Lmorganizer@yahoo.com*) is an experienced professional organizer. She is a friendly, frank person who inspires confidence. Meyer says her clients are not dysfunctional, they are just busy. "We are talking smart, smart people. They will follow a system. I pay one person's bills for her. Oftentimes it is more of a maintenance issue with them." Her client told her, "I know I can do this, but it will go faster with you here."

Snow says, "With packrats and hoarders, you want to be creative. You want to help them make good decisions. There are different approaches. Some don't let me touch their stuff. Basically what I do is help them sort it out and we go through piles and piles. I let them take breaks and I go sit in another room." She sometimes has to take the discarded items (and trash) away from the premises to keep the client from reclaiming it. She has observed that one sign of true hoarders is that they are sleeping on half or less of the bed.

"I use gadgets," Snow says. "I gave one client one of those gag gifts, called 'the birth control pill,' that when you squeeze it, you hear a baby cry. When he didn't want to get rid of something, he touched it and it was his release. I give eulogies for an item that a client can't give up. It worked well for one client. It helped her get over the hump. I try to find something they can identify with. I give them a different analogy depending on their interests."

Snow doesn't believe in buying a lot of unnecessary containers. "I try to utilize what they have the best I can. I don't run out and get containers. Containers are not always a solution. They are often a way of avoiding the problem. An old shoe box works fine."

Snow is another who believes that "You can change your lifestyle. It all depends on what is important to you."

All the organizers I spoke with agreed that organizing is a process. You can't finish in one day. There is going to be some disarray before your home is livable space.

Success Means Changing Patterns

"If I see them two days later and my work has been demolished, I almost take it personally. Most of the time these slips happen because they don't want to get rid of the stuff. They are being forced to."

—Diane Snow

Success can be defined as getting a person decluttered and giving them tools they can use to stay that way after the organizer leaves. Although none of the organizers kept hard statistics, most agree that with motivated clients, the success rate is high. With severe clutterers or hoarders, it is harder to say, as most organizers don't often get to see the finished project. Money is often the issue. Severe cases can run into thousands of dollars.

Meyer put it pithily, "Success depends on how much they are willing to throw out."

Linda Durham, owner of Organizing Matters in Houston (281-304-0695; *www.organizingmatters.com/*; e-mail: *OM@organizingMatters.com*), is a bright, cheery person who got into organizing after finding her way out of being a clutterer herself. Her goal in life is to bring hope to others in the same sinking boat she escaped. "I am living proof of change," she says. Durham believes that her success rate is very high because her clients "feel so marvelous and free once they get started that they are off and running. I do myself out of a job! Most of my clients are really, really behind. I give them a leg up and they run with it."

"[There is] something else that I find key to my clients' success," says Durham. "Once it is established that he or she wants change, it is my job to help them in many ways. I am a resource to them for physical help with clutter, I recommend books, supplies, and products that work for my client in his/her situation to assist them in reaching their goal of success. As we work together I find that a serious clutterer *has had their common sense misdirected through years of bad habits and procrastination.* As we work, I redirect their common sense by helping them see they have too much of something or that something could be moved to a place that would serve them better."

Durham does not believe that you can change a lifetime of habit in 21 days or some other arbitrary number. "I have a habit of twirling my hair. I will be watching TV and be surprised to find myself twirling my hair. I have never been surprised to find myself cleaning a toilet," she quips. As she sees it, staying decluttered is a choice, not a habit. "You have to retrain your thinking. It's a choice you make every day. You've got to reshape that pattern."

"We are creating hope by the minute. One of the things I love about my job is that we are creating hope," says Durham. I have to agree, as just talking to her would give hope to a dead man.

Organizers Know There Are Different Types of Clutterers

Professional organizers have learned to categorize clutterers, hoarders, and packrats. Snow put it like this: "The hoarder has a serious problem and can't let go. He sees garbage as worth. A packrat is different. They just seem to have too much—too many clothes for example. I don't hold fast to 'If you haven't used it in a year or two, throw it out.' We all have a bit of procrastination. But at some point we need to get rid of something. You have to be realistic with people. You have to go with the way they function and they work. In our business there is a lot of hand-holding. You have to be tough, too."

Meyer also works with hoarders. "Some of the hoarders I meet with every week. I find there is a lot of fear behind the clutter. As long as the clutter is in their life they don't have to move on. It is like they are trying not to get ahead. I highly recommend they get into therapy. There are all kinds of excuses why they can't declutter."

One client called Meyer saying she wanted to redecorate. "But the real issue is that she lives on a trust fund and is 39 years old. She doesn't know how much money is coming in. I can't get her to a financial planner. I finally got to the root. 'Why can't we throw things out?' I asked. 'If I throw it out I will feel guilty,' she said. She buys a lot of little stuff and that little stuff adds up. She clips coupons to save 50 cents and if she went to a financial planner she could make it up in a minute."

Meyer says that the elderly, mostly in their 60s, are not necessarily more difficult. "Some people are ready to change habits [at any age]. Some aren't. In my case it is the elderly who call, not their families. The average age group of my clients is in their 40s and 50s."

Most of the organizers I spoke with agreed that hoarders present the greatest challenges. Snow put it like this: "It can be very difficult and wearing working with a hoarder. They fight you tooth and nail. They need the help because of outside influences. Consequences happen because of their hoarding."

Unforeseen Effects of Helping a Hoarder

One elderly woman collected garbage. Though she was wealthy, she brought home garbage. She literally collected it from dumpsters. My own mother developed this habit as her Alzheimer's Disease progressed. Though it is very difficult to understand why an Alzheimer's patient does anything, I believe that her convoluted thinking had connected it with my father. When I was growing up, we were very poor and my father and I would go to the county dump to reclaim furniture or other odds and ends that we might be able to use. This organizer's client could not give a reason for her actions, other than "these things have value." She saved all her hair from her hairbrushes. Her house had gotten so filthy that she was asked to move. She was feeling invaded because her family was nagging her to clean up.

Snow said that the "success" of the decluttering was questionable. The woman had been talkative and outgoing in her old place. She took the bus to town every day. "Once we got her cleaned up and moved into a new place she spoke to no one and went in to a deep depression. There was a huge change in her personality. It is a dilemma. Do we let them live out their lives as they want?"

Another woman refused to throw anything out. She had a chair that couldn't even stand by itself. Hoarders see value in things that others don't. She couldn't bring herself to throw it out. Even the usual technique of taking a picture of the chair wouldn't convince the woman to part with it. Snow tried to reason with her. To the woman, it had worth. "People would actually pay money for this chair," she told the organizer. "People would pay big money for that." Snow recalls that the chair was not an antique, it was just an old chair. She adds, "Don't even ask about the conversations we had about a table with a top as wavy as a Pringle!"

Even a professional, for whom the hoarder (or his family) is paying good money, cannot always convince him to part with cherished objects. In cases like this, it is good to have a therapist involved, because the issues are much greater than chairs or tables.

Professional Organizers and Therapists

Snow says, "We are not therapists. We are here to organize. We would like to work as a team [with the therapists]. The therapists often do not know the full extent of the problem. Sometimes they don't know what we are talking about." Of her clients who had therapists, she has never talked to the therapist, but she has suggested that clients bring up the issues that they encounter when trying to declutter.

Lynn Meyer, owner of All About Time in Chicago (e-mail: *Lmorganizer@yahoo.com;* 312-222-1856), said, "Therapists have recommended me. I will tell a client 'talk to your therapist about this,' when issues come up."

Snow says, "It is sad that lots of people who need us can't afford us. Some people think it should be covered under insurance. If someone has OCD, why wouldn't the help to get over this be covered?"

Durham puts it like this. "Sometimes a PO has to cut loose from a client. We might find we can no longer help them for different reasons. Also, it is our moral responsibility to direct that client to a better match. It may be another organizer or it could be an ADD counselor or even an OCD specialist. I have only had to let one client go. Within our work together, we discovered that she had a tremendous debt load, of which she was unaware. I kept working with her to get her organized enough to go to a debt counselor. I refused payment and agreed to help her again after she worked with a financial counselor."

Emergency? Don't Call 911, Call Your Organizer!

People tend to call in organizers because of some traumatic catalyst. Once they decide they need to get rid of something they have to do it right away. Sometimes health officials have been called in. Or the hoarder is threatened with losing his or her apartment. One frantic woman called an organizer because her apartment complex was going to do an inspection. The organizer told me, "I've gotten a lot of calls due to the landlord having come into the apartment and announcing 'Clean it up or move out.'"

Snow had a young woman call saying, "Help me, it is an emergency." "I changed my plans and went to her," Snow says. "The emergency was she couldn't keep a boyfriend because of the way she kept her bedroom and bathroom. She told me, 'I've got to do something about this.' She was young, beautiful, athletic, had a good job. She had three big garbage cans she used for clothes hampers."

Meyer says, "When somebody calls me it is not because things are a little bit messy. It is because it is a disaster. If I can walk into a room without having to climb over junk, I feel like there's hope. Unfortunately, it has taken as much as five hours to find the top of a desk."

Choosing an Organizer

Finding an organizer can be as simple as going to the Yellow Pages and looking under "Organizing Services." One really nifty site with many links to organizers around the world is the Professional Organizer's Web ring (*www.organizerswebring.com*). Or you could go to the NAPO Web site, listed earlier. If you have a therapist, he or she might be able to recommend an organizer.

Choosing an organizer is a bit more difficult. Trust—both financial and emotional—is a very big issue. You need to ask what their credentials are, how long they have been working, and what their specialties are. Membership in NAPO is a good sign, but that doesn't mean that someone who is not a member isn't reliable. Organizing is a home-based business in many cases. A number of years in business is a good indicator, but everyone had to start out sometime. Being bonded is a sign that the person has bought an insurance policy to cover them-selves, but many good organizers are small businesses and the cost of bonding is prohibitive. I believe that it is a matter of finding the right personality to match yours.

On the emotional side, you should pick an organizer the same way you would pick a therapist. Ask her how she would deal with certain things that are bothering you. Is she going to be able to straddle the line between being effective and still honoring your feelings? Is her style regimented, with a philosophy that you should only handle a piece of paper once, or throw away anything you haven't used in a year? Or is she flexible enough to adapt to the situation? And which do you want? Most of us have reasons, no matter how illogical, for holding onto cer-tain items. How are we going to deal with the emotions attached to discarding those items because someone else says we should? On the other hand, we don't want someone who will let us keep every item we have. We might as well not hire them if they are too wishy-washy. We have to have reached a point where we want to change in order to hire an organizer, just as we have when we choose a therapist. We want some-one who will help us out of our morass gently.

Trust Your Organizer!

Trust is paramount. As Linda Durham says, "within one hour a professional organizer *will find something personal and private that should stay personal and private.* Even the purest among us has personal infor-mation that should stay personal. A good professional organizer will know that and honor it. Integrity within the profession is crucial. That is also where personal referrals are important. Even if a client finds me 'cold', it is my job to earn his/her respect and trust.

"I have an agreement that I ask my clients to read that helps them trust me too. In addition to my breakage/replacement promise, I also make sure that my client knows that we can each fire each other for any reason at any time. That way, if things get too personal, there is always an out."

Diane Snow echoes this sentiment. "We know everything there is about you," she says. "We know your finances, your hiding places." I understood this within minutes of having Diane Ridley, owner of Home in Harmony in Los Angeles (626-799-7003) in my house. With my fiancée standing right there, she uncovered my box of pictures and love letters from old sweethearts!

But there are also people who give an organizer the keys to their house and just tell them to get at it. These people are ready for a general to go in and take the field. In this case, the financial trust issue comes up.

Snow sums it up as follows: "You can tell by the way people are watching you where their trust level is. Everything is confidential. Many of the clients will give me the keys to their homes and let me come and go." On the issue of references, she said that some people will give you a referral and some won't. Some are still ashamed for having needed an organizer in the first place. Oddly enough, thanks to Oprah and the publicity that cluttering has gotten lately, some people now see having an organizer as a status symbol, akin to having a personal trainer!

The Inside Stuff Changes, Too

Organizers agree that the problem is not just the clutter they encounter. They understand that the inner clutter is what caused the outer clutter. One told me of two ladies who called her in because they wanted to move to Florida. They may not be able to do that because they are not willing to do what is necessary to get there. Their clutter is a way of not making a decision. Another said, "Clutter is not just clutter, any more than food is just food or sex is just sex. There is a reason for these things causing problems."

I was surprised to find that the organizers I talked to echoed my earlier sentiments on spirituality and clutter. Durham expresses it succinctly. "I am a person of faith and faith *is* hope," she says. "Several years ago, my life changed when I got organized. That is why I do what I do for a living. Getting organized was something God gave me that I share with others."

Meyer echoes the metaphysical principle that making room for new things to happen in your life makes new things happen in your life. "I don't know how all this works," she says, "but when people clear out their clutter, new, positive things appear in their lives. I had a client who cleared up her closets and the man of her dreams showed up. I find this kind of thing happens all the time to my clients. I find that what's on the outside is a reflection of what's going in the inside. Happens every time."

Meyer believes that her clients come to her through synchronicity. When I asked her how people find her, she replied thoughtfully, "I believe there is a spiritual side. The people who call me fit. When a person is ready there is an attraction. They attract the right people to help themselves. I have the right skill sets. When the student is ready the teacher will appear."

21 | Clutter and the Workplace

"Corporate clients aren't attached to their clutter. Lawyers don't cry over the papers shredded."

—Lynn Meyer, professional organizer

Most clutterers have to work somewhere. Some of us are able to control our cluttering in the workplace and present a relatively organized facade. This can be like the alcoholic who doesn't drink during working hours. He may not be drunk at the office, but you can bet that his problem is affecting his performance. It is easy to identify a clutterer as someone who has a messy desk, but many people have messy desks and can find whatever they need in seconds. Also, with so much information computerized, it is easier to hide clutter. A resourceful clutterer will be able to stall until he has found a lost computer file, blaming it on a network error or computer glitch. Linelle Wilson, a perceptive service manager for national accounts working with Fortune 500 companies says she spots closet clutters by their chronic missing of deadlines and being late for conference calls. "Every employee has unique strengths and weaknesses. My job as a manager is to help them develop their weaknesses into strengths."

My original intention for this chapter was to interview personnel directors and managers. However, it quickly became apparent that, as one top-level executive coach said, "They haven't a clue." Their approach is usually to send the employee to an organizing seminar and implement some directives about to-do notes, or something along those lines. However, if you have a clutterer in your organization, and he is worthwhile to your company, it will take a lot more than that.

The businessperson who clutters is more common than generally acknowledged. Although there are few diagnosed hoarders in this category, messy, disorganized executives, middle managers, and frontline employees cost American businesses an untold amount of revenue.

Lost Time = Lost Sleep = Lost Functionality

One aspect of cluttering that comes into play in business is lost time. When a disorganized employee spends time shuffling through papers or e-mails to find documents he needs to do his job, he is using time that could be spent on new projects. How much of the 60-hour workweeks so common today can be attributed, at least in part, to cluttering?

Plenty, according to Dr. Donald Wetmore, president of the Productivity Institute, a seminar company (60 Huntington St., P.O. Box 2126, Shelton, CT 06484; 800-969-3773; e-mail: *ctsem@msn.com;* Web site: *www.balancetime.com*). The institute's time management and personal productivity seminars have been taught to dozens of major corporations, from ABC-TV to Westinghouse, and all the letters in between. Wetmore says, "Studies have shown that the person who works with a messy desk spends, on average, one and a half hours per day looking for things or being distracted by things. That's seven and a half hours per week.... And it's not a solid block of an hour and a half, but a minute here and a minute there...like a leaky hot water faucet, drip, drip, drip, it doesn't seem like a major loss, but at the end the day, we're dumping gallons of hot water down the drain that we are paying to heat."

Getting "Caught Up" Instead of Sleeping

According to a *U.S. News and World Report* cover story (Oct. 16, 2000), many working Americans are operating on a permanent sleep deficit. According to the story, Americans have a "cumulative national sleep debt of 105 billion hours." Getting less than eight hours of sleep a night weakens the immune system, which encourages colds and further erodes productivity.

Scientists used to believe that we could make up our sleep deficit in a fairly short period, but recent research indicates this is not so. One study showed that it took three weeks to make up a 17- hour sleep deficit, although another indicated that two eight-hour sleeps could suffice. Other side effects of a lack of sleep are a decrease in levels of cortisol, which is common in elderly people. The result: you look older. And if that's not enough, sleep loss also produces a decrease in levels of the hormone leptin, which increases the body's need for carbohydrates. Result: increased eating and weight gain.

One study showed that "people who stay awake for up to 19 hours scored worse on performance tests and alertness scales than someone with a blood-alcohol level of .08 percent—legally drunk in some states." According to Richard Gelula, executive director of the National Sleep Foundation, "Driving while drowsy is no different than driving under the influence of alcohol or drugs." Some experts believe that our national sleep deficit contributes to the national epidemics of obesity and diabetes.

Commuting and Telecommuting Pitfalls

With the advent of telecommuting and the ability to work at home comes the tendency to think, "If I don't get finished this afternoon, I'll work late tonight and get it done." Before I got fired from my last real job with a company, management saw having me telecommute as a solution to my messy office. I guess they figured, "Out of sight, out of mind." Although it did give them a more presentable office without me in it, my lack of time management expanded my working day to 15 hours—all to accomplish what I used to do in eight. My favorite time to e-mail projects to the office was 3 a.m. Unfortunately, I had to take calls from customers at 9 in the morning, so my sleep deficit mounted rapidly.

The middle manager leaving the office long after his employees have gone home, and then carting a bulging briefcase, is the norm rather than the exception. Because so many of us are on the road, spending four out of five days traveling between cities to do our work, it is inevitable that we lose sleep. To do business, we need to catch early flights for one city and late-night flights to another. Even the most organized person is challenged under these circumstances. Combined with the stress of traveling, many of us suffer from a lack of restful sleep. The clutterer is hardest hit trying to adjust to these circumstances. We spend extra hours doing the things we didn't get done in the first place or waste precious time looking for our misplaced plane tickets and hotel directions, packing and unpacking our disorganized suitcases.

The Clutterer as Road Warrior

Most clutterers struggling to perform jobs that require a lot of travel will identify with my experiences on the road. When I was a guidebook author and photographer, I used to travel by car for two to five weeks several times a year. Fully three days before I left, the other employees in my office avoided me as they would a bear with a wounded paw. I became frantic, searching through files, trying to find valuable information I needed to update. My understanding boss finally banned me from the office a day before my departures.

That didn't help. It took that day and most of the next day and night to get my clothes ready and my truck packed. At the last possible minute, I threw everything I thought I might need into at least three suitcases. It took at least four false starts before I had returned home to pick up something I had forgotten. One time I actually made it to Mexico without my cameras! At each stop I was burdened with gear, filling up the dresser and tabletops with open suitcases. I had to rummage through everything to find anything and of course it only got worse as the trip proceeded. Half the time the company had to fax reams of information to me because I had forgotten important papers.

When I flew to speaking engagements or book signings in the States, things got worse. Limited to two suitcases and a carry-on, I suffered even more stress than usual as I tried to fit as much as possible into a smaller space. Clutterers are indecisive. I couldn't decide what clothes to wear, so I just dumped the clean clothes hamper into a suitcase and sat on it to close it. My laptop case bulged with files and books I thought I just might possibly need. In 13 years of this kind of traveling, I do not recall ever getting to bed before 3 a.m. the day I was scheduled to leave. Because I lived in a small town and had to catch a 6 a.m. flight to connect with the world, I often didn't really sleep for fear of over-sleeping. Fortunately, I was able to sleep on the plane, thanks to ear-plugs and a sleep mask—if I'd remembered to bring them.

Once I was the national spokesperson for a company I'd rather not embarrass. My speaking and public appearance schedule was very tightly packed. I'd do three or four TV, radio, or newspaper interviews in a city in the early morning, then fly off to another city to make the evening news. Like any road warrior, I came through when the pressure was on and managed to appear relaxed and intelligent before the cameras. But it was a miracle. The worst time was when I woke up in a darkened hotel room and the clock said 4:30. I didn't know whether it was a.m. or p.m. I didn't know *where* I was. I honestly didn't know *who* I was. A puzzled desk clerk told me I was in Phoenix and knew my name. It was morning, and I was scheduled to do a 5:30 a.m. radio interview. That was close!

Sleep Deficit a Side Effect of Cluttering

According to the National Sleep Foundation, "One half of the American work force (51 percent) reports that sleepiness on the job interferes with the amount of work they get done, 40 percent of employees admit that the quality of their work suffers when they are sleepy, and nearly one out of five (19 percent) report making occasional or frequent work errors due to sleepiness, suggesting that the nation's productivity is not as high as it could be if Americans got more sleep." Catherine Jewell is a performance specialist in Austin, Texas (512-255-1255; *www.jewellspeak.com*). She is a freelance trainer for corporate environment soft skills and managerial training time management. Jewell agrees, "People are sleep deprived and pressured at work."

Time Management Can Help

If you have employees who are clutterers, you are going to have to call out the big guns instead of the one-day seminars. There are three main options. You can hire a professional organizer who specializes in corporate work, you can hire a performance specialist, or you can send them to an intensive seminar for time management. Actually, a combination of all three might be called for, and may benefit all employees, not just the clutterers.

Catherine Jewell took the Franklin Quest course in 1993 and is still using it. She likes to implement the Franklin Day Planner time management system. Some companies are mandating a specific organizing system through e-mail. They use only one system, which includes personal commitments with professional commitments, based on the theory that you've got to see how your whole life plays out for the week in order for your planner to be effective. Catherine has written a book, *31 Days to a Better Boss: Ways to Stop Whining, Start Planning, and Take Charge of Your Career Today,* which can be helpful in learning new techniques.

Disorganization May Signal Other Problems

"When I teach Covey's 7 Habits of Highly Effective People, taught one day a week for three weeks, people reveal a lot about themselves," says Jewell. "The number one issue is a struggle to maintain a home life and a work life. They feel guilty about not being the parents they want to be. Sometimes their marriages are falling apart because of all the above."

Jewell says that with tools for proper time management and goal setting, people can overcome these drains on their business and personal lives, as well as their health. "I have met some extremely organized, capable people who seem much less stressed because their lives are organized," she notes. "They have boundaries, and they are assertive. I know a young man who is working in an environment where 50- to 60-hour weeks are the norm. He works 40. And he's been promoted three times in three years. Maybe it's matter of focus."

Jewell gives seminars and works with major corporations like Dell Computers, Southwest Airlines, and Chase Bank on the issues of time management and goal setting. "I work with mangers to get the best from their people. I work with individuals to find their life's inner passion....Sometimes it is a change of workplace. Sometimes people don't need to be trained just to be given better tools or better motivation."

Changing corporate environments have also contributed to clutter by causing disorganization. Jewell finds that "everyone is a little bit" cluttered and disorganized. "What I've seen in a lot of corporate environments is a lot less storage space," she notes. "Where before people had six drawers, now they have two." Because of this, files tend to get crammed together without an organized filing system. Managers need to hang on to important documents but they don't have the room for lots of file folders, so papers get filed in a general file where it is impossible to find them quickly. When the important documents are needed, time is lost shuffling through others that *might* be important some day.

"There is a lot of movement within the corporate environment in general," Jewell says. "People move six times in four years. Because of that, many people do not have a reasonable filing system. So they remain disorganized until the move. Then they can give themselves permission to discard files." That is when all the CYA files get disposed of. People are aware of this and thus don't have to own up to their disorganization.

Sometimes professional organizers have to take a back door approach and ask about people's personal lives in order to help them. Sometimes their cluttering is a reflection of their dissatisfaction with their work. Meyer spoke to a national professional organization and the conversation kept getting back to people who were unhappy with their jobs and careers. "There ain't no time management in the world that will fix that," she observes.

Not Dysfunctional, Just Busy

Lynn Meyer, owner of All About Time in Chicago, is a professional organizer who works with corporations. She gets hired for professionals who are bringing work home and for whom the office has spilled over into their entire lives. "Then they travel like banshees," she says. "They don't have a system and it totally gets away from them. They are not dysfunctional, just busy." Often the employees feel like they are drowning and that the boss has thrown them a lifeline. "There are times when I go in and the employees are so happy that the boss will pay for this," Meyer says.

Clutterers Can Be Like Alcoholics

Sometimes, however, Meyer meets with resistance. Her most important advice to employers who want to help cluttering employees is what not to do. Typically, she is hired by a "boss who calls me in and wants me to fix that person. I go in and meet with the employee. 'I don't have a problem,' is a common response. Resistance is monumental. They are balking and will do the opposite to spite you. What I have found is it is almost like an alcoholic. They have to admit they have a problem [and say] 'This system isn't working for me.'" Meyer approaches the employee in denial with an is-there-anything-I-can-help-you-with attitude. She's found that most people come around when they don't feel that they are being singled out or threatened.

Some employers have suggested that their employees attend self-help groups like Clutterless, or a 12-step program like Clutterer's Anonymous. Whether this will help or not depends on how it is presented, and of course, on the employee's motivation. I have known people who were recommended to treatment centers or Alcoholics Anonymous by their bosses for whom the results have been truly amazing. Other times, it was wasted effort.

In my case, when I was impersonating an executive at a major international bank, my boss very kindly suggested that our insurance would pay for a treatment center to help me with my drinking problem. Outwardly, I said I would consider it, but inwardly, I thought, "I knew it! This is a way of getting rid of me. He wants to get me out of the office for a month and then hire someone else. Then there will be this big black mark on my personnel record. I'll show him! I'll find another job." And I did. A year later, the courts forced me to go to AA. I was still resentful but had no choice. I went. It took. I stayed. So you never know.

At Clutterless meetings, there have had been some members who were referred by their bosses. The bosses explained that this was like an on-going seminar and a tool to help the employee improve his performance and personal life. Since it is not a 12-step "anonymous" program, they were less resistant to it. In most cases, they have stayed and their job performance (and lives) have improved. But, in cases where the boss said, "Go to these meetings or get out," the results were less than satisfactory.

It is important for bosses to understand that Clutterless meetings are not time management courses or places where people go to get tips on cleaning out their drawers. Although specific decluttering issues may be addressed during a meeting, the focus of the group is to deal with the emotional and spiritual limitations that cluttering causes. Clutterless meetings are not a Band-Aid, they are gentle surgery. They augment the work of professional organizers, therapists, and time-management professionals, but they do not replace them.

Different Approaches for Different Types

If you have a variety of personnel types working for you, a cookie-cutter approach will not work. People who are artists, like graphic designers in advertising agencies, aren't going to have pretty little stacks. They won't respond to the same organizational tools as those in the accounting department. Moreover, just because something *looks* disorganized doesn't mean it is.

If you can find something at a moment's notice, you are not disorganized. Time management is a tool. If you are spending time looking for things, you need a tool to help you stop wasting time. Some people have messy desks and can find things. Some people are very neat and can't find anything.

As a reformed clutterer, I personally disagree with the one-system-fits-all approach. Some systems will make sense to people and they will use it if they are motivated. Forcing a company-wide system that doesn't fit the individual will just cause some of us stress and resentment. But I am probably outnumbered here. If your company can tolerate employees picking systems that work for them, at least try it. I like using a computer program called Maximizer as my organizer and personal information manager. It just makes sense to me and has a feature that others didn't have when I was choosing which one to go with; it can search by first name, and I am more likely to remember someone's first name than last. Most companies use ACT! or Goldmine, or another popular brand. I have tried them all and found that Maximizer works better and makes more sense to me. My productivity would suffer from the resentment caused by having to use a program that I thought second-rate. My dedication to performing is enhanced when I feel I have some choice in making decisions. As long as your employees are not using this as an excuse to avoid changing their cluttering behavior, why not let them use what works for them?

Disorganization Affects CEOs, Too

Jewell says, "I see disorganized people at all levels. I've seen administrative assistants who are picking up the pieces for their CEOs." Wilson agrees that most executives would be lost without their secretaries.

Meyer works a lot with CEOs. Her background was that of an executive secretary with a major hotel organization and later a consulting firm. "When the boss is disorganized they are leading the team. Teach them how to work with their secretary. There is a lot of creativity and leadership in CEOs. They are not necessarily detail people. I tell them, 'You're supposed to be leading a corporation and you are working out of a sticky pad? You run your corporation with a business plan, but how about your personal life.'"

Outsource Your Personal Life

According to Meyer, some companies, especially consulting firms, do recognize the stresses that extensive traveling places on the personal lives of their employees. One company she worked with, Anderson Consulting, has a concierge service for employees who travel. The concierge service outsources their personal life. When one executive had a car break down, for example, the concierge picked it up. "If you are organized," she says, "traveling is still difficult. If you are disorganized, you are sunk."

Jewell advises traveling businesspeople to streamline their personal lives. "Pay your bills electronically. Hire a lawn service that comes regularly, so you don't have to call them. I used to have seven phone bills and now I have two or three. One thing I do is hire a money coach to pay all my bills."

Meyer says, "I liken myself to a personal trainer. We all can exercise. When you are not doing it, you hire a trainer." She considers it her role "to keep them going. Going through paper is the last thing they want to do after they go on the road. They tell me 'If you weren't here, I would never do it.' I give homework. People respond to the word homework. 'Your homework is to finish this drawer.' I give them three things they've got to do. 'Buy three containers. Finish this drawer on the left.' Very specific."

Focus

Sometimes, clutterers may find they just don't fit in a certain environment. It may not be our fault. Our apparent disorganization is a way of rebelling against being forced to be round pegs in square holes. If this is the case, all the time-management systems and seminars will do little to enhance our lives. While we may become apparently better employees, our personal lives suffer. At some point we have to learn to focus on what is really important to us and take the action to follow through. If you find yourself resentful of having to do things a certain way, and are self-aware enough to know that it is not because you *can't* do it the suggested way, but rather that you *don't think it makes sense*, then you may have some hard choices to make.

Edison, Einstein, Thoreau, and Jesus Christ all questioned the status quo and did things their own way. A popular advertisement encourages us to "Think outside the box." If you're feeling like you are inside a box and unhappy, then maybe you just don't fit where you are. There is a place for every one of us to express our unique talents, gifts, and personality. Just because a corporation says it has the right way to do things, doesn't mean it is right for you. If you have honestly tried to apply the principles in this chapter to your work life and find it is causing you more stress than ever, maybe there is another answer for you, somewhere else.

Valuable employees are hard to keep. If you can find reasonable ways to accommodate the corporation's needs with your personal needs, present it to the powers that be. Life should be lived with passion, not desperation. (My goal in writing this chapter was to help all those who want to do jobs they love more effectively.) It was not to make anyone feel they have to conform for conformity's sake.

I asked everyone I interviewed for this book to define the difference between a workaholic and someone who loves to work. From psychiatrists to ministers to organizers to time-management consultants, it boiled down to this: If you find passion in your work, then your work is play. If you are working to get by and to pay the bills, if you have lost your personal life and get no joy from your job, you are a workaholic. Losing a job is not the end of the world. Losing yourself to a job is.

When we eliminate clutter from our lives and minds, we learn to live our lives fully. Anything else is a waste of all our efforts, an affront to the God-self within us. May you find your path and follow it.

22 | When You Slip

We have made a long journey together. I hope I have helped you in some small way to free yourself from your prison of clutter. I hope you have gotten yourself to a place where you can move freely, think clearly, and feel proud.

If you are a real clutterer, like me, this is an unnatural situation. Your normal life pattern is to create chaos and mess wherever you go. You are breaking old patterns of behavior that took years to create. It is possible that you will revert to the old way of doing things when you are sad, depressed, anxious, or complacent.

Clutter Slowly Creeps Back

No one is perfect. After you have decluttered, you will feel great. Then, slowly, it starts. A newspaper is left out. Dishes go unwashed.

One book for nighttime reading is left on the bed. Then his pals join him. Then they have a party and invite their friends. Before you know it, you are overwhelmed again. Don't panic. This is the time for support from other clutterers. This is the time to put into practice the principles you learned about why you wanted to live clutter-free. Unlike when an alcoholic or drug addict has a slip, it is probably not life-threatening. Remember that—it makes it easier to handle. A slip is not the end of the world. Slips are also easier to deal with because you don't have as much stuff as when you started. Accept that you are not perfect and get back to work. Your new life is worth it.

Talk. Take Responsibility. Take Action.

The first thing to do is to call another clutterer and talk about it. If you have a therapist, talk about it. If you have joined Clutterless or Clutterer's Anonymous, go to a meeting. If you don't live in a town with a meeting, start one. Helping others gets us out of ourselves and into recovery. Visit the Clutterless Web site, *www.clutter-recovery.com*. Ask for support and information on how to start a group in your town. There are clutter discussion groups on MSN and other online services. Talk to a friend. The worst thing you can do is ignore your clutter. It wasn't put there by fairies. You created it. Take responsibility, but don't take blame. Then take action.

When this book was close to completion, I had a major slip. Of course, I rationalized that I did it on purpose so I could add to the book. (My God, does the rationalization ever stop?!) Like all things that have happened in my life, it happened for a reason. I learned from it, so in that sense it was a good thing. That story constitutes the last chapter. I will tell you how I felt and how I dealt with it spiritually, emotionally, and practically.

Visualize and Get Vision

Remember the meditation you did when you first started to declutter? Did it help? Well, then, do it again. Visualize yourself living in a clutter-free house. Visualize yourself confident and proud and able to take care of the problem. Read the affirmations in this book. Make up your own.

Now get out the pictures of your house before you started to recover, and compare them to your house as it is now. Chances are, it is nowhere near as bad as it was. Pat yourself on the back. You've come a long way, baby. You don't have that far to go to get back to where you were. All you have to do is to start. You can do it, but no one else can do it for you. If you start, others will help you. If you wallow in your misery and clutter, you will sink back into the quagmire. The choice is yours. May God help you with the right choice.

Reasons for Slips

Let's see why you might have slipped. Like an alcoholic, who didn't just wake up drunk one day, you didn't just wake up cluttered. Certain behaviors and thoughts led to your cluttered state. You chose to abandon the lifestyle that made you feel good for one that was comfortable. You left your new lover for the old one. Why? Only you can answer that for yourself, but here are some possible reasons. If you recognize the thoughts leading up to this negative action, you will be able to stop them in time the next time...or the time after that.

My problems aren't that serious, my stuff is just out of control

That fits most of us when we have a slip. We let one thing go and it doesn't seem that bad. Like many alcoholics or drug users who have slips, we may find that we can handle one or two. But like them, our addiction sneaks up on us and before we know it, we are overwhelmed.

It may start in your bedroom, your sanctuary. You can still invite others to your house, just not there. Then it is the coffee table. Then the living room. Then it is just all too much.

If you can, start picking up where you started putting down. If trying to remember where you started will slow you down, start anywhere. No matter where you start, or when you start, just start! The task isn't as daunting as you think it is. Only you make it so. You can do it.

A major trauma

A loved one died or left you. You left a loved one. Your beloved pet died. These are awful events and you are entitled to grieve, or to be angry. But is your cluttering going to bring them back? If it is someone who died, and you loved them, don't you think he or she would want you to have a clutter-free life instead of retreating into clutter as a way of mourning?

If it is an ex-lover who set you off, is your living in depression going to help you get even with him or her? If you start making your own life miserable, aren't you giving that person power over you? Do you really want to give that person the power to ruin your life again?

You will love and be loved again. If you are emotionally healthy and clutter-free, your chances are greatly improved. Give yourself a break, give yourself a chance, give yourself your life back. Get back on the program.

As you begin to clean up the wreckage of your present, toss some stuff. Start with those things that remind you of the one who is gone. If you hate the person now, view it as throwing him or her out of your life. If you lost loved ones, view it as helping them move on. If you love them, you still have the memories. If you hate them, get rid of any objects that could trigger memories.

What happens if you reconcile? They will either understand or not. If they don't, that is their problem, not yours.

You went on a trip and left a mess

This happens a lot. Before you go, you put your house into disarray when you are packing. You don't have time to clear it up. You live out of a suitcase while on the trip. When you get back, it's hard to unpack. The suitcase lies on the floor. You rummage in it for stuff. You get used to walking around it. The other stuff in the house never gets put away. More stuff ends up on the floor.

This is typical. So many of us have to travel for business today that it's hard to keep up with any kind of routine. Often after a trip, whether business or pleasure, I was disoriented for about a week. When I surfaced, clutter had reared its ugly head. I have vowed not to let that happen again. Now, I get the suitcase unpacked within a day or two.

Start with the suitcase. Toss the brochures that you don't really need. File the papers you do need. Wash the dirty clothes. Ditch the plastic hotel sacks they were in. Return the suitcase to where it lives.

Then get busy on the rest of the room, and then the rest of the house. Remember, this is a minor setback compared to where you have been.

Financial setbacks have paralyzed you

This happens to all of us. A business deal didn't work out. You lost your job. The Stock Market went down. You had unexpected expenses from an illness, a child's illness, home repairs, car trouble, and so on. This is life. It happens to everyone.

First of all, get your financial house in order. Figure out your true financial situation. Not knowing is scary. It leads to mental clutter. Clear off your desk and get out the checkbook and the bills. If you are seriously behind, do what normal people do—sell something, cut back, get a part-time job. Make a plan to get out of the financial mess. With that off your mind, you can start working of getting rid of the physical mess.

Money flows. It cannot flow to you if your life is cluttered. Give it a chance.

It just happened

Bull! Living clutter-free lost its priority. You left a newspaper out until you got a chance to read it. You were going to clip an article from a magazine on your coffee table. You left the dishes undone. You didn't put away the groceries. You bought something new and didn't discard the box. You, you, you. Get the picture?

You did it and you can undo it. Start with the newspaper. Forget the clipping. Put away the groceries. Just get started and great things will follow.

Nothing matters anymore

Depression happens. You are in a fog, nothing has meaning, and you don't seem to have purpose anymore. You feel worthless, so why care? You wonder if anyone cares what happens to you. Your life is such a mess on the inside that it's very hard to care about the outside.

But you do have purpose and someone does care, even if it is only I. What is going on in your physical realm *is* happening in your mental realm. If you take action in one, the other will follow.

Pets can help

If you have a pet, you have a perfect depression reliever. If you have a cat, she will love it if you stay in bed all day. You can comfort each other. Your dog will try to talk you out of it. Snakes and fish aren't much help, though your boa might hug you. Birds seem to understand when you talk to them about it. They at least pretend to listen.

Talk

I have suffered from major depressions, even to the brink of suicide. So I know that when we are in that frame of mind, we cannot use the tools we have. If you have a therapist, make an appointment. Then hang on. Don't take the permanent solution to a temporary problem. If you feel you can't afford a therapist, there are community services that can help you. There are crisis hotlines you can call. Your clutter buddies will listen. You are not alone, though you may feel that way.

If you can't do it on your own, seek professional help. God gave psychiatrists and psychologists their gifts to help people like us. Good ministers are there to help their flocks through trying times. Call yours.

Read

Read something. Some of us can't deal with anything more challenging than mystery novels when we are down. But if you can, try some uplifting books. Whether you pick up something by Tony Robbins or the Dalai Lama, pick up something. Stop listening to depressing music. Stop looking at the news. Rent some funny movies. Stop worrying about the whales, global warming, or the devious Republicans or Democrats in Washington. You may be able to do something about those things when you are your old self, but right now, you need to get yourself together.

This is not for everyone, but a visit to the General George S. Patton Jr. Web site might get some of us motivated: *http://members.aol.com/ PattonsGHQ/homeghq.html.*

Take Action

If you do nothing else, pick up your clothes off the floor. It will help you as much as a therapy session. You are in control of your stuff, not the other way around. Don't give up. I want you around to buy my next book. Don't let me down, okay?

Write a letter. Express your feelings without reserve. Put all your anger, fear, self-pity, loathing, pain, and any other emotions you have into it. Hold nothing back. Then, on a new page, write any solutions you can think of. If you can think of nothing better, just put "better." Write down what you would like your life to be like. Be as optimistic and positive as you feel you can be at this time.

Then take the letter outside into the sunlight, to the beach, to the mountains, or wherever you feel is a blessed place. Hold it in your hand and say something like, "Here, God (or Buddha, Tao, Jehovah, Great Spirit, Universal Intelligence, or whatever your Higher Power is called), please take these things. I can no longer deal with them. I give them, and the solutions, to You." Feel the release as you say these things. Then burn the letter. As it goes up in smoke, feel that your blackened spirit is being burned out of you too. I always feel a great sense of peace after doing this ritual. I hope you do too.

You may feel an immediate release, or it may take days. But it will come. Upon your return home, try to not pick up the problems you just burned. Get busy when you get home and throw one thing out. Pick up and put away one thing. If you have a spiritual program, start it again.

You didn't get into the woods in one giant step, and you won't get out of them in one giant leap. Just start walking and looking for that sunlight at the end of your dark trail.

23 | My Last (?) Slip

"Behind every beautiful thing, there's been some kind of pain....I just don't know why I should even care. It's not dark yet, but it's gettin' there."

—Bob Dylan

This book was nearly finished when I slipped. My house had been impeccable for several weeks. I washed the dishes after each meal, cleaned my desk and filed my papers every evening. I made the bed and dealt with the laundry in an orderly, neat manner. I, I, I. Maybe that was the root of the problem. Maybe I forgot that I alone do nothing, that a Higher Power enables us to do the things that keep us on track.

My slip started with the bedroom—just like I had written in the book. Before I knew it, the back door was blocked by baskets of clothes, both clean and dirty. A big box of stuff I intended to go through was in the middle of the floor. Still, I took pride in my desk and dishes. I rationalized the messy bedroom because I was tired when I quit my 16-hour days, and after all, I was the only one who saw it.

Then the dishes were left undone one day. I was tired. I felt that washing them every day was an obsessive habit. I was no slave to habit.

How did it make me feel? At first, I felt like I was in control. I controlled whether things would be cleaned up. I was not living a rigid life. I was free of external compulsions. About the same time, I decided that my morning meditation was taking too long and shortened it. Nightly prayers of thanksgiving seemed to be superfluous.

The front room got littered with newspapers. Instead of throwing them away, I pushed them aside so I could eat at my table. When I had rearranged the room weeks before, I'd put all my videos into a suitcase so I could move the entertainment center. The suitcase was still there.

Although I usually get by with five hours of sleep, I was grumpy and edgy. I didn't seem to think as clearly. My business suffered. My financial clarity came crashing down. When I went to write a large check, the bank informed me I had only $4,000 in my account. I thought I had $12,000.

The desk was clutter's last triumph over me. I remembered a boss who 30 years ago insisted I stay late to clear my desk. I vowed that I wasn't going to let him control me anymore. I would show him! I doubt that leaving my desk in Galveston a mess was going to have any effect on him, but when we are slipping, we aren't logical. I rationalized that I was busy; I had Web pages to build, a database to fix, and a business to run.

Guess what? Building the Web pages and fixing the database took longer because I couldn't find the materials I needed on my littered desk. Some of the links on my pages didn't work because my thinking was jumbled and I made silly mistakes.

The final straw was that I stubbed my toe on a box in the middle of the night. I had prided myself on being able to walk through my house in the dark. Now I was back to irregular paths.

I Made a Call

I told all this to Samantha, a fellow clutterer, and she reminded me that we should not beat ourselves up, that we are not perfect. That helped me stop feeling guilty and start doing something about it.

The next morning I had to wash the dog dish. After all, my dog depended on me. Then I wanted some espresso. The pot and maker were dirty, so I had to wash them. While I was at it, I remembered what I had written about dishes not taking that much time. By golly, what I wrote was right! It didn't take that long. I cleaned the counter while I was at it, and that mess I had dreaded for so long took about 20 minutes to eliminate. I felt good, clean in soul and spirit.

But old habits come back easily and it is hard to break them. That night, I stayed up until 4 a.m. and was too tired to make the coffee for the next day. In the morning I dreaded going into the kitchen. My previous joy at starting my day with fresh coffee was replaced by disease. I stayed in bed, but I prayed for clarity. I petted my dog. That always helps when I am down.

While the espresso maker hissed and frothed, I congratulated myself on at least getting the kitchen clean the day before. I had done at least one thing right. I should have read my own book!

Meditation Helps

Espresso in hand, a fresh cigar in my mouth, I went to the tub and began my meditation. I meditated in a Buddhist sense, not concentrating, but feeling the words, "clear mind." It was one of the best meditations I have ever had. My limbs literally floated away and I became more in tune with my higher purpose. Some great writing followed.

Things are getting back to normal, or at least what is now normal for me. I took out the trash and cleaned the desk, and I keep on working. Maybe having that slip and writing about it enabled me to better share my experience, strength, and hope with you. We often put writers on altars and think of them as more than we are. I remember Leo Buscaglia once saying that he got too many hugs whenever he went out. He couldn't get any peace. He was only human. So are we all.

My slip reminded me that I am only a man, a vessel. I have no wisdom of my own making. Whatever I have shared with you has come from you and from the spiritual ether. Only when the vessel is open at both ends and the truth can flow through me to you can I be free. If it is blocked, I am doing the blocking. When one area of my life is blocked, all areas of my life are blocked. There is a quotation from the Bible on my desk. My slip reminded me that I had forgotten it. May you not.

"Draw near to God and God will draw near to you."
—James 4:8.

Appendix

Clutterless Statement of Principles

© Clutterless (used by permission)

Clutterless in Seattle, or New York, or Galveston, or Houston, etc. is a self-help group for people who think they might have a problem with clutter in their lives: physical, emotional, spiritual. We are not a 12-Step program, but a self-help program that operates on practical, spiritual, and psychological principles. We are groups of people who get together and focus on clutter as an impediment to living successful, happy lives. We have only one 12-Step tradition and that is that we respect the anonymity of all who attend. We realize that cluttering is often shame-based and we are here to help, not foster that shame.

All are welcome. If you believe that disorderliness or clutter is causing you problems, no matter how great or small, you are welcome. If the clutter of another family member is causing problems, you are welcome. If you are only a little disorganized, you are welcome. If you are a diagnosed hoarder, you are welcome. We are all in the same boat. Together we can paddle upstream. If we remain isolated, we will all drift aimlessly.

We leave all decisions about therapy to the individual. For some of us, it is a solution that works. Others of us may not be ready or feel like we need it. Our focus is on helping each other as only others who have the same affliction can do.

Professionals from the helping professions, such as psychiatrists, psychologists, counselors, ministers, and professional organizers are welcome to attend meetings and are given time to discuss their ideas of treatment or methods of helping. Most of the meetings are taken up with discussions among the clutterers themselves, similar to group therapy. No cross-talk is allowed in this part of the meeting, as the meetings should provide a safe environment to be heard without comment.

Meetings start with a focused meditation. We use this time to get in touch with our God or Higher Power, whether it be Jesus, Bhudda, Tao, Moses, Yahweh, Nature, Spirit or any other name you choose to give to Him or Her. Our focus in meditation is on orderliness and thankfulness.

We believe that the individual is an expression of God's love and God wants us all to live happy, joyful, orderly lives. We believe that each of us is successful and perfect in our own way. We may just need to realize this and learn to express our success to ourselves first and to the world secondly. Our success and self-worth do not come from people, places, or things. They are outward expressions of our inner perfection. We seek to unlock that expression.

Please join us at *www.clutter-recovery.com* or write to Clutterless World Headquarters, 1116 Ave. L, Galveston, TX 77550-6135 for information. Please include $5 to defray expenses and include a large self-addressed, stamped envelope with 77 cents postage.

Resources

Web Sites

www.clutter-recovery.com
Homepage for Clutterless self-help groups. Has ideas for dealing with clutter in our lives, a discussion forum, and information on starting a Clutterless group in your city. Very uplifting.

www.ocfoundation.org
Homepage for the Obsessive-Compulsive Foundation. A wealth of information and literature for dealing with OCD.

neuro-mancer.mgh.harvard.edu
A great site for medical discussion groups about hoarding and dozens of other topics. Operated by Massachusetts General Hospital. (Note that there is no "www." in this address.) It can also be accessed via *www.braintalk.org*.

www.clutterers-anonymous.org
Homepage for Clutterers Anonymous, a strictly 12-step approach to recovery.

www.recovering-couples.org
Homepage for RCA (Recovering Couples Anonymous). This is an excellent program for couples who are in recovery of any kind and wish to apply the 12-step principles to their relationship.

Organizations

Clutterless
1116 Ave. L
Galveston, TX 77550-6135

Clutterless meetings provide a safe place to be heard, discussions of ways to get out of the clutter trap, and practical suggestions. Clutterless considers its approach, which includes meditation, prosperity thinking, and common sense, "practical spirituality." For a meeting schedule, information on organizing chapters in your area, and pamphlets specifically for clutterers, send $5 and a large SASE with 77 cents postage.

Clutterers Anonymous
PO Box 91413
Los Angeles, CA 90009-1413

CLA is a 12-step group specifically for clutterers, based on the principles of Alcoholics Anonymous. Send a large SASE for information.

The OC (Obsessive-Compulsive) Foundation
PO Box 70
Milford, CT 06460
(203) 878-5669

The definitive source of information about OCD and its treatment. Sells many books on the subject. Very helpful. They operate on donations and memberships, so please be generous if they help you.

Obsessive Compulsive Anonymous
PO Box 215
New Hyde Park, NY 11040
(516) 741-7401

This 12-step group is for people diagnosed with OCD symptoms, including hoarding. Send a SASE for an information packet.

Bibliography

Ash, Mel. *The Zen of Recovery*. New York: Penguin Putnam, 1993.

Brink, Susan. "Sleepless." *U.S. News and World Report*, 16 October 2000.

C., Roy. *Obsessive Compulsive Anonymous: Recovering from OCD*. New Hyde Park, N.Y.: The Obsessive Compulsive Foundation, 1997.

"City Cleans Filthy Condo." *Milwaukee Journal-Sentinel*, 28 August 1997.

Fox, Emmet. *The Sermon on the Mount: The Key to Success in Life*. San Francisco: Harper San Francisco, 1989.

Gillis, Anne Sermons. *Offbeat Prayers for the Modern Mystic*. Spring, Texas: Easy Times Press, 1998.

Hay, Louise. *Love Yourself, Heal Your Life Workbook*. Carlsbad, Calif.: Hay House, 1990.

————. *You Can Heal Your Life.* Carlsbad, Calif.: Hay House, 1999.

Holmes, Ernest. *Science of Mind.* Marina Del Rey, Calif.: DeVorss and Company, 1995.

————. *Living the Science of Mind.* Marina Del Rey, Calif.: DeVorss and Company, 1997.

Holtzman, Liah. *Forgiveness Equals Fortune.* Scottsdale, Ariz.: L.H. Publishing, 1998.

"In a Town of Eyesores, a Boat Is a Thing of Beauty." *The Wall Street Journal,* 26 January 1999.

Jampolsky, Gerald G. *Love is Letting Go of Fear.* New York: Bantam Books, 1998.

Jewell, Catherine. *31 Days to a Better Boss: Ways to Stop Whining, Start Planning, and Take Charge of Your Career Today.* Austin: Copyright Success Address Press, 2000.

May, Rollo. *The Meaning of Anxiety.* New York: Washington Square Press, 1979.

"More Than 100 New Laws Take Effect." *Savannah Daily News,* 29 June 1998.

Obsessive Compulsive Disorder: A Survival Guide for Family and Friends. New Hyde Park, N.Y.: Obsessive Compulsive Foundation, 1993.

Orman, Suze. *Nine Steps to Financial Freedom.* New York: Crown, 1997.

————. *The Courage to Be Rich.* New York: Riverhead Books, 1999.

"Packrats May Suffer From Disorder, Experts Describe Causes, Treatments." *Long Beach Press-Telegram,* 14 August 1994.

Peale, Norman Vincent. *The Power of Positive Thinking.* Englewood Cliffs, N.J.: Prentice Hall, 1978.

————. *The Amazing Results of Positive Thinking.* Pawling, N.Y.: Peale Center for Christian Living, 1987.

Phillipson, Steven. "The Right Stuff: Obsessive Compulsive Personality." *OCD Newsletter,* 4 January 1999.

Ponder, Catherine. *The Dynamic Laws of Prosperity.* Englewood Cliffs, N.J.: Prentice Hall, 1962.

————.*The Dynamic Laws of Prayer.* Marina del Rey, Calif.: Devoss and Company, 1987.

Rappoport, Judith L. *The Boy Who Couldn't Stop Washing.* New York: Signet Books, 1991.

Robbins, Anthony. *Unlimited Power.* New York: Fawcett Columbine, 1987.

Schwartz, Jeffrey M. *Brain Lock: Free Yourself from Obsessive-Compulsive Behavior.* New York: ReganBooks, 1986.

"Software Pioneer Dead at 37," Associated Press, 22 April 2000.

Steketee, Gail, and Teresa Pigott. *Obsessive Compulsive Disorder: The Latest Assessment and Treatment Strategies.* Kansas City, Mo.: Compact Clinicals, 1999.

Van Noppen, Barbara L., Michelle T. Pato, and Steven Rasmussen. *Learning to Live with OCD, 4th ed.* New Haven, Conn.: Obsessive Compulsive Foundation, 1997.

Index

About
the
Author

Mike Nelson has been featured by the *Los Angeles Times* and CNN for his work with cluttering. He was instrumental in the founding of the Clutterless self-help groups. A reformed clutterer himself, he works with other clutterers and shares his knowledge, strength, and hope through speaking.

A prolific writer and speaker, Nelson has been an international newspaper columnist, has published a dozen books, and has given keynote addresses in the United States and abroad. As the former spokesman for the Mexican Tourism Office, he educated the public about travel in Mexico through speaking engagements and media interviews throughout the United States, Canada, and Mexico. He has received international media attention from such publications as *The Wall Street Journal*, *The New York Times*, *Texas Monthly*, the Manchester (England) *Guardian*, and the *Mexico City News*.

Writing as "Mexico Mike," Nelson has guided several thousand people through every part of Mexico. Some of his work can be viewed at *www.mexicomike.com*. In addition to writing, Nelson owns and operates an Internet-based wholesale travel agency, Spa World Reservation Service (*www.spagetaway.com*). Nelson's business background includes banking, insurance, hospital administration, and options trading on Wall Street. Born in Las Cruces, New Mexico, he has lived all over the United States and Latin America. He currently lives on Galveston Island, Texas.

Also by Mike Nelson:

Live Better South of the Border

Spas and Hot Springs of Mexico

More Than a Dozen of Mexico's Hidden Jewels

Mexico's Pacific Coast

Mexico's Ruta Maya

Mexico's Colonial Heart

Mexico's Gulf Coast and Costa Esmeralda

Central America by Car

Mexico From El Paso to Mazatlan

Mexico From the Driver's Seat

The Sanborn's Travelog

Sanborn's Guide to Fishing Mexico